CHIEF JOSEPH

Candy Moulton

THE AMERICAN HEROES SERIES

Amelia Earhart: The Sky's No Limit by Lori Van Pelt
Chief Joseph: Guardian of the People by Candy Moulton

FORTHCOMING

John Muir: Magnificent Tramp by Rod Miller
Mary Edwards Walker: Above and Beyond by Dale L. Walker
David Crockett: Hero of the Common Man by William Groneman III
George Washington: First in War, First in Peace by James A. Crutchfield

Dale L. Walker, General Editor

CHIEF JOSEPH

Guardian of the People

CANDY MOULTON

A Tom Doherty Associates Book
New York

CHIEF JOSEPH: GUARDIAN OF THE PEOPLE

This book is printed on acid-free paper.

Map by Mark Stein Studios

Book design by Michael Collica

*Frontispiece photograph by John H. Fouch,
courtesy of Dr. James S. Brust*

A Forge Book
Published by Tom Doherty Associates, LLC
175 Fifth Avenue
New York, NY 10010

www.tor.com

Forge® is a registered trademark of
Tom Doherty Associates, LLC.

Library of Congress Cataloging-in-Publication Data

Moulton, Candy Vyvey, 1955–
    Chief Joseph : guardian of the people / Candy Moulton.—1st ed.
        p. cm.—(American heroes series)
    "A Tom Doherty Associates book."
    Includes bibliographical references and index (p. 223 and
p. 231).
    ISBN 0-765-31063-5 (acid-free paper)
    EAN 978-0765-31063-7
    1. Joseph, Nez Percé Chief, 1840–1904. 2. Nez Percé Indians—
Kings and rulers—Biography. I. Title: Chief Joseph. II. Title.

E99.N5M68 2005
979.5004'974124'0092—dc22
[B]

                                                        2004056318

First Edition: March 2005

PRINTED IN THE UNITED STATES OF AMERICA

0 9 8 7 6 5 4 3 2 1

To my parents, Fox and Betty Vyvey

Contents

Contents

Foreword

O f all the many fading signposts of the Old West that illustrate the struggle between Indian and white for supremacy over the lands between the Mississippi and the Pacific coast, none can compare to those marking the journey of Chief Joseph and his band of Nez Percés in the summer and fall of 1877.

Joseph's story, like all great epics, is filled with irony. The Nez Percés had befriended Meriwether Lewis and William Clark when the explorers crossed the continent in 1805 and emerged from their journey across the Bitterroot Range starving and exhausted. The high country Indians, magnificent horsemen and a handsome, healthy, and intelligent people, fed the expedition dried buffalo meat, camas root bread, and fish, taught them to make sturdy canoes by burning the hollowed-out tree trunks, gave them good directions to continue their way west, and pledged their friendship to the white men who would be arriving in their wake.

In the spring of 1806, the Corps of Discovery, now heading east on its homeward journey, stayed with the Nez Percés in the Kamiah Valley almost a month waiting for the snow to melt so they could cross the Bitterroots. During this period, Captain Lewis explained the trade alliances and peace proposals that the White Chief in Washington, Thomas Jefferson, wanted submitted to every tribe the expedition encountered. The Nez Percé headmen watched the sign language the translators used and found the ideas agreeable. All they asked in return was to trade with the whites for guns so they could compete with the neighboring Blackfeet for buffalo and defend their villages.

On July 26, 1806, two months after departing the Nez Percés, Lewis and two expedition members were camped with a party of eight Blackfeet Indians on the Marias River in northeast Montana. The parley was cordial at first but quickly turned hostile when the Blackfeet decided to make off with the Lewis party's horses. As a result, this only armed encounter with Indians during the entire expedition left two of the Blackfeet dead and opened a century of bitter conflict and the eventual herding of the West's native populace—including the Nez Percés—onto reservations far from their homelands.

The Nez Percés tried valiantly to live up to their end of the promise of peace and accord with the white intruders. Chief Joseph's father even followed the white man's road for a time, learning of Jesus and the Bible in a missionary school and taking a Christian name for himself and his son. Old Joseph eventually returned to the traditions and religion of his people, but the Nez Percés remained true to their pledge.

It could not last. Worthless treaties, lying commissioners and Indian agents, land-hungry settlers, belligerent military commanders—mostly simple broken promises—ended a peace that had endured for over seventy years, and led to the rising of the Nez Percés, the rise of Joseph's son as guardian of his people—the epic contained in this book.

Central to Joseph's story, indeed, the allegory of his life's pursuit, is the zigzagging flight he led between June and October 1877, guiding 750 of his people from the Nez Percé homeland in the Wallowa Valley of northeastern Oregon to the Bear's Paw Mountains, forty miles from the Canadian border with Montana. Author Candy Moulton calls this 1,500-mile journey the Nez Percé "hegira," a good word choice—the original Hegira depicting the flight of Muhammad from Mecca to Medina in A.D. 622 to escape persecution—and has re-created it in heartbreaking detail: Joseph, his band of brothers, their wives, children, and elderly kinfolk fleeing a frontier army of infantry and cavalry under some of the toughest Civil War–tested generals of the era—O. O. Howard and Nelson A. Miles chief among them, with the army's commanding general, William Tecumseh Sherman, issuing killing orders from behind the lines.

Candy Moulton has walked the ground Joseph and his people walked, has followed their trail from the Wallowa Valley of Oregon through Idaho and Montana, including Lapwai, the Spalding Mission, Camas Prairie, White Bird Canyon, Dug Bar, Kamiah, the site of the Clearwater battle, Weippe Prairie, and over the Lolo Pass. "I've been at the site of Fort Fizzle, through the Bitterroot Valley, at the Big Hole battlefield several times," she says. "I've camped on Bannock Pass, been across the Camas Meadows and to the site of the fight there, where rock fortifications used by the troops remain in and around a small tree grove. I've been over Targhee Pass and through Yellowstone, horsepacked to the Lamar River country over Mist Creek Pass and through the Pelican Valley, been in the Sunlight Basin and along the Clark's Fork River in northern Wyoming several times, attended the commemorative events at the Battle of the Bear's Paw and Big Hole, and traveled in northern Montana and southern Saskatchewan to sites where Sitting Bull had his camps during his exile there."

The power of the Nez Percé hegira has not diminished in the 127 years that have passed since it took place, the author says: "Lodge poles in place but without their coverings at the Big Hole in Montana seem to represent the tranquility of any Indian village, but as I walked across this battlefield on the first of several visits, the spirits of the eighty-nine Nez Percé men, women, and children who were slaughtered in the early-morning raid of August 9, 1877, seemed to rise up to meet me in the sounds of wind rustling the grass and a hawk keening as it soared above. In the quietness of this site I realized that what I heard is what Joseph's people heard, too, in those final moments before gunshots pierced their lodges and bodies. But the wind and the hawk reminded me that people may die, but spirits do not. The power of the land pulled me strongly at the Big Hole, seeming to surge with energy from the Nez Percés whose bones remain here, far from home, but never forgotten by their people."

Moulton's portrait of Joseph is of an intricate man, both perplexing and enlightening to his people and to his white friends and foes. He was admired for his philosophical eloquence, his nobility as Nez Percé guardian, his steadfast pacifistic beliefs, and, for a peace chief, his brilliance as strategist.

Significantly, three of Joseph's adversaries, none given to after-the-victory honoring of their enemies, nor to romanticized ideas of the Indians they fought in the western wars, were of a rare single voice in remembering their 1877 campaign and their opponents.

General of the Army W. T. Sherman lauded Joseph and the Nez Percés, calling their flight "one of the most extraordinary Indian wars of which there is any record."

Colonel Nelson Miles, a Medal of Honor veteran of wars against Comanches, Kiowas, Cheyennes, Sioux, and Apaches, had a special respect for the Nez Percés, referring to them as "the boldest men and best marksmen of any Indians I have ever encountered." Of their leader he said, "Chief Joseph is a man of more sagacity and intelligence than any Indian I have ever met."

And the most relentless of Joseph's pursuers, Major General Oliver O. Howard, the deeply religious one-armed Medal of Honor hero of the Civil War, abolitionist, and advocate of black suffrage and later of Indian rights, told the Nez Percé leader after the war ended, "You, Joseph, will show yourself a truly great man, and your people can never be blotted out."

—Dale L. Walker

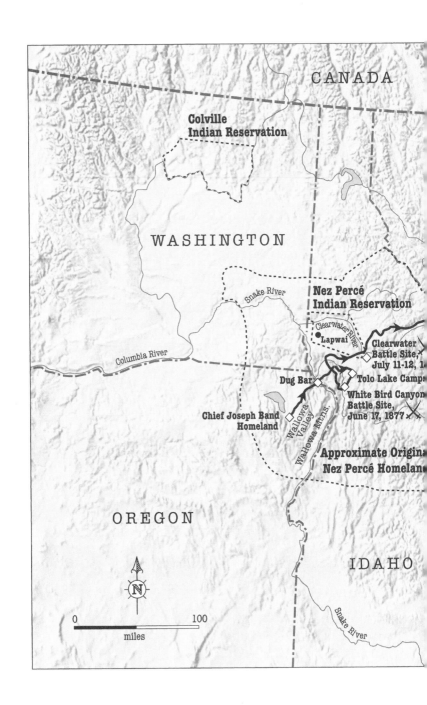

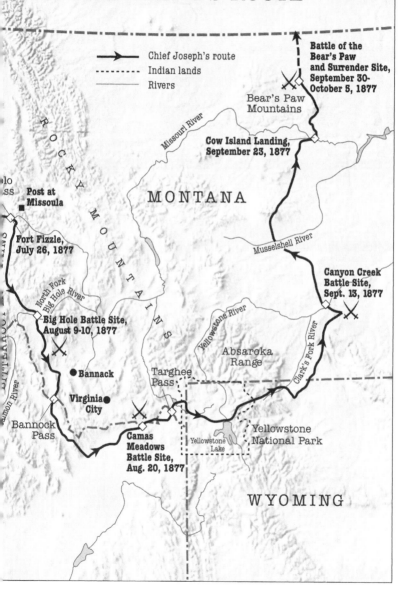

CHIEF JOSEPH'S ROUTE

→ Chief Joseph's route
---- Indian lands
— Rivers

Battle of the Bear's Paw and Surrender Site, September 30-October 5, 1877

Bear's Paw Mountains

Cow Island Landing, September 23, 1877

Missouri River

MONTANA

Musselshell River

Canyon Creek Battle Site, Sept. 13, 1877

Post at Missoula

ROCKY MOUNTAINS

Fort Fizzle, July 26, 1877

North Fork Big Hole River

Big Hole Battle Site, August 9-10, 1877

Yellowstone River

Absaroka Range

Clark's Fork River

Salmon River

● Bannack

Targhee Pass

Virginia City ●

Bannock Pass

Camas Meadows Battle Site, Aug. 20, 1877

Yellowstone Lake

Yellowstone National Park

WYOMING

CHIEF JOSEPH

Prologue

A cold wind swept across the northern plains that October morning in 1998 when, at the invitation of the Nez Percé* elder holding a smoking calumet, several men and one old woman took their places in a circle. Younger Indian women pulled brightly colored shawls close to their bodies and formed a semi-circle around those seated. The elder motioned to those of us who were not Nez Percé and said, "Join us. We welcome you." Nearly 200 years earlier, in 1805, Nez Percés fed starving American explorers William Clark and Meriwether Lewis before showing them how to build canoes from pine trees and providing detailed information about their route to the Pacific.

There is a long history of welcome from Nez Percés to outsiders.

The crisp air carried the hint of snow forty miles to the

*From the French for "Pierced Noses," the name is pronounced "Nez Purse."

north in Canada. From the hill where we stood, it seemed so close to that border, yet for the Nez Percé people who had been at this site near the Bear's Paw Mountains of northern Montana Territory in 1877, that distance meant an eternity in exile and the demise of their free-ranging lives. Now, as they gathered at Bear's Paw on the anniversary of the battle, those in the circle passed the pipe, smoking or lifting it in reverence to the spirits, to honor ancestors, and in humility and in pride of their culture.

Children played in the grass sometimes laughing aloud and young mothers or solemn grandmothers hushed them until, hearing their outbursts of joy, the elder told the women to let them play and laugh. Once, at this place, Nez Percé youngsters cried in fear, suffering from bitter cold temperatures, wind, snow, and wounds from soldiers' bullets. "Let them laugh," the elder said. That simple statement, quietly uttered more than 120 years after the flight of the Nez Percés, seared itself into my soul, and though I have since traveled to other battlegrounds along the route Joseph and his people took in 1877, no one image is so etched in my mind as the thought of children unable to laugh and play for fear they would be shot when all they wanted was to live free in their homeland.

The Nez Percés were an adaptive, progressive tribe responsible for development of the Appaloosa horse and reliant upon free-flowing streams, native plants, and wildlife herds for their food and shelter. In 1831, they sent emissaries to St. Louis, inviting Christian missionaries into their land to bring them the power they associated with the Bible. Nine years later, in the high Wallowa Valley of northeastern Oregon,* a Nez Percé woman gave birth to the child who would become Chief Joseph. Leadership was not hereditary in this tribe, but a young man from a powerful family, such as Joseph, could attain a headman's role if he exhibited strong leadership skills. Joseph lived at a Christian mission, learned to speak English, and studied the Bible until age seven, when his father withdrew from Christian influence and reverted to traditional Nez Percé belief: the "Dreamer" religion in which men and women lived from the bounty of the land, roamed freely throughout their territory, and received guidance from spiritual visions.

Joseph was fifteen when his father signed a treaty that he believed preserved the tribal homeland. The older man prepared a parchment map and set stakes around the Wallowa Valley to signify his claim to it. Eight years later government officials presented to him a new treaty that significantly reduced the size of the reservation and took from the tribe Joseph's homeland. His father refused to sign that treaty, as did several other Nez Percé headmen. These leaders, all Dreamers, now "non-treaty" chiefs, split their own nation in two—at a time when civil war embroiled the Americans—leaving only the "treaty chiefs," all Christian believers, to sign the document. Under Indian belief no headman's individual decisions bound any other headman, but federal officials said the signatures of the treaty chiefs obligated all Nez Percé

---

*Throughout this book I make reference to present-day states' names and other places to orient the reader. Of course, during the early period of Joseph's life these boundaries did not exist.

leaders to the 1863 document's provisions. That meant, without their consent, the "Dreamers" lost much of the tribal ground.

Joseph assumed his father's role as headman for their Wallowa Band of Nez Percés not long after the 1863 treaty council. For the next dozen years he led the people through the quagmire of governmental negotiations, relying on diplomacy to preserve his homeland and in the process becoming the best known of Nez Percé anti-treaty leaders. Federal investigators agreed with Joseph's claim that his territory had not been relinquished, President Ulysses S. Grant issued an executive order that restored their homeland to the Indians, and governmental officials recommended removal of encroaching white settlers. The United States Congress, however, rescinded Grant's order, and as a result the whites stayed and pressure mounted to relocate the Nez Percés, as had already been done with dozens of other tribes.

In 1876, the ill-fated U.S. Seventh Cavalry command of Lieutenant Colonel George Armstrong Custer attacked a much larger force of Lakota and Cheyenne Indians camped along the Little Bighorn River in Montana Territory. The killing of Custer and his troopers led to a nationwide demand that all free-ranging Indians be forced onto reservations, and this outcry set the stage for the events of 1877 that made Joseph a nationally known figure.

During four months of conflict involving a flight of 1,500 miles to elude various army units, Joseph emerged in the nation's newspapers, and to the pursuing military commanders and troops, as the supreme war leader of the Nez Percés. Then, and for fifty years afterward, he was recognized as the great Nez Percé war chief who had—with babies, women, and old people in tow—outfoxed, outmaneuvered, and out-fought a great federal army.

In reality, Joseph was not a war chief; that task fell to his younger brother and other Nez Percés. Instead, he had a far more important role during the hegira: he became the guardian of the people, eventually becoming their sole spokesman, and when exiled to Indian Territory, this man who had pledged to "fight no more forever" immediately launched a campaign for better conditions for the Nez Percés and all Indian people. He lobbied Congress and presidents, military commanders and Indian Bureau officials to return to his homeland, winning his battle in the court of public opinion by enlisting the support of Christians and Indian reformers.

Joseph assumed the mantle of leadership from his father but won the respect of his people and an admiring public for his oratorical skills and tactical achievements. He became a hero not for his battle planning and prowess as a fighter but for his diplomacy and his example as a man of humanity, respect for people of all backgrounds, and, most of all, unfailing love of freedom and homeland.

He Had Sharper Eyes

The old man's eyes were clouded with age, but his vision had not failed. "My son," he told the strong young man who held his feeble hand, "my body is returning to my Mother Earth. My spirit is going very soon to see the Great Spirit Chief. When I am gone, think of your country."

There had been more such advice and instruction about dispensation of his property in that final message from father to son, from an old headman to a young one, who both used the same white name: Joseph. "You are chief of these people. They look to you to guide them. Always remember that your father never sold his country. You must stop your ears whenever you are asked to sign a treaty selling your home," the old man said in a rasping voice. "A few years more and white men will be all around you. They have their eyes on this land."

Already the weight of responsibility had settled upon the heir; he had spoken for his father at council and had become the recognized leader of the Wallowa Band of the Ni-mii-pu, the Nez Percé, as the whites called them since the first French-Canadian trappers saw the dentalia shell ornaments in their noses.

As his father's breath and spirit fled, Hin-mah-too-yah-lat-kekt absorbed the final words deep into his soul: "Never sell the bones of your father and your mother."

The Nez Percés believe they were created by Coyote as he cut and ripped apart the monster living in the Columbia River Basin, then used pieces and parts of the monster's body to create the tribes of the Cayuse, Umatilla, Walla Walla, Spokan, and others. When Coyote got to the heart, all that was left of the monster, the heart had turned to stone and became a bump on the land at Kamiah, beside the river that eventually took the name Clearwater. Coyote had nothing left except the blood upon his paws, which he washed with water. Drops of this water touched the soil and the Nez Percés believe their tribe emerged from the blood spatters. They call themselves The People—Iceyeeye niim Mama'yac: The Children of the Coyote.

Coyote gifted them with strength and wisdom. They would rise above the other tribes in the region by developing power and intellect and wealth. When the horse was introduced into their lands in the early 1700s, they were not content to simply ride the animal; instead, they watched nature's cycles and took steps to improve the breed, castrating inferior animals and breeding strong stallions to fertile mares. Their horses, the forerunners of the Appaloosa breed, had strength and speed and marvelous colors ranging from blacks and browns to pure white, with spotted rumps and deep-barreled chests. They became war horses—wealth, and mobility, for a nation.

With the horse the Nez Percés spread across their lands, separating into bands that ranged through the Columbia Basin from the central and northern mountains of Idaho and western Montana to the valleys of northeastern Oregon and southeastern Washington. There were many leaders, wise men who had learned from their grandfathers, as was their tradition, or sometimes from fathers and uncles. There were strong, brave young men and women who herded the horses, made periodic forays to the buffalo country along the Yellowstone River far to the east, and gathered the nutritious camas lily from the prairies where it grew in natural flower beds that shimmered like a lake when the blue flowers were in full bloom from July through September. In early spring they collected misshapen white kouse roots from other meadows and netted, speared, or trapped salmon during the annual runs when the fish swam up the deep waters of the Columbia to the swift flows of the Snake, Clearwater, and Salmon rivers that crisscrossed Nez Percé lands.

But times were not always so tranquil. The Nez Percés had enemies, including the Shoshones, called Snakes by white men, who made their homes in southern Idaho and western Wyoming, and the Blackfeet from the country along the Canadian border in north-central Montana. Sometimes the enemies came into Nez Percé country, attacked the People, and took captives. Such was the fate of one woman abducted by enemy raiders and taken far to the north and east. After much time away from her people she gave birth to a child, then escaped her captors and began making her way back to her village. The child died on the journey, but the woman, now called Watkuweis (Returned From a Far Away Country), safely reached her homeland.

This woman's experiences had great meaning for the young explorers William Clark and his co-captain, Meriwether Lewis. When their Corps of Discovery struggled across the Bitterroot Mountains in 1805, subsisting on horseflesh and little else, Clark and some of his men walked out of the deep forest and onto a high plateau area, the Weippe Prairie, on September 20, and saw Indian lodges across the open country. Clark wrote in his journal: "[A]t the distance of 1 mile from the lodges, I met 3 Indian boys, when they saw me [they] ran and hid themselves." He stopped his horse where the youths had crouched, handed his gun to one of his men, and then searched through the tall grass until he found two of the boys. Clark said he gave them "small pieces of ribin & Sent them forward." The boys fled to the village of fifteen or so lodges made of poles set in a conical shape and covered with bark mats. Soon a man approached the explorers and ushered them into a lodge where they were fed buffalo meat, dried salmon, berries, and roasted camas roots, which Clark thought tasted like onion when made into bread or soup.

Before the explorers actually reached the Nez Percé village, arguments had broken out among the People. Some suggested that the interlopers should be killed, but the former captive, Watkuweis, now an old woman, spoke on Clark's behalf. She told her people how the whites she had met near the Great Lakes to the east had helped her during her years of captivity. She argued for the safety of the exploration party. Her people listened, fed Clark and his men, and later assisted the explorers as they made their way down the high plateau and steep mountainside to the fast current of the stream Clark and his men thought the Indians called the Kooskooske, the *koos keich keich*—clear water.

Alongside the Clearwater River, Clark found the village of headman Twisted Hair, to whom he presented an Indian peace medal bearing the face of President Thomas Jefferson. Meriwether Lewis, meantime, traveling behind Clark with some other members of the Corps of Discovery, also eventually reached Weippe Prairie, where he handed out more tobacco, trinkets, medals, and two American flags. Lewis and his party also descended the mountain and soon joined Clark at Twisted Hair's village. They remained there until October 7, during which time they felled massive Ponderosa pines and learned from Nez Percé men how to burn and scrape the logs and turn them into dugout canoes. They left their animals in the care of men from Twisted Hair's village, pushed the canoes into the Clearwater, and began the last leg of their journey to the western rivers—the Snake and the Columbia—and eventually to the Pacific Ocean.

The Indians watched over the horses and goods the explorers left behind and the next year, when the captains returned to the Nez Percé camp on the Clearwater, they found welcome and assistance once again. Because they had departed their dreary, damp winter camp at Fort Clatsop near the Oregon coast earlier in the spring than they should have, the explorers arrived among the Nez Percés too early in 1806 to continue traveling east—the tribesmen told them they could not cross the rugged Bitterroots for many days because snow was too deep in the high country and there would be no grass for the horses. The Corps of Discovery thus waited at the Nez Percé village until the season advanced enough for them to venture on.

"Those people has shown much greater acts of hospitality than we have witnessed from any nation or tribe since we have passed the rocky Mountains," Clark, in his shaky syntax, wrote in his journal, ". . . in short be it spoken to their immortal honor it is the only act which diserves the appellation of hospitality which we have witnessed in this quarter."

Lewis also remarked on the Nez Percé hospitality, citing the promise of one tribal elder who told them "the whiteman might be assured of their warmest attatchment and that they would alwas give them every assistance in their power; that they were poor but their hearts were good."

The dominant tribe in the region had made a clear and distinct choice: It would do no harm to white people and would provide them assistance.

Of course, the tribal leaders of 1806 had no inkling how many whites would eventually come tracking across the nation and into Nez Percé country.

David Thompson, a thirty-one-year-old geographer and mapmaker, introduced the Montreal-based fur-trading North West Company to the Nez Percés in 1807 when he established Kootenai House on the Upper Columbia in southern British Columbia. The trading post was far north of Nez Percé territory but not too distant from one route the tribe regularly took along the Clark Fork River to hunt buffalo in Montana. At Kootenai House Thompson exchanged tobacco, awls, and guns manufactured in London and Birmingham, England, for beaver and bear furs, horses, and dried salmon brought in by the Nez Percés.

In New York in 1808, German immigrant John Jacob Astor founded the American Fur Company, eventually sending two parties to the Pacific Northwest. One group sailed on his ship, the *Tonquin*, with a cargo of trade goods, traveling around Cape Horn to the mouth of the Columbia, where the Astorians established a fur-trading post. At the time the *Tonquin* departed New York, Astor agent Wilson Price Hunt scouted overland routes to the Columbia. His party dumped its canoe into the raging whitewater of the lava-lined walls of the Snake River on the Idaho–Oregon border and they survived by eating mountain goats and beaver as they struggled along the steep, rock-strewn Snake canyon to the Salmon River, where some Nez Percés found them. As with the Lewis and Clark party, the Indians fed and provisioned the Astorians before sending them on their way.

Astor's toehold on the Oregon coast soon collapsed and he sold out to the Nor' Westers, soon to be in a cutthroat competition with Hudson's Bay Company, the powerful British fur-trading operation. In 1821, the French and British companies merged into one fur powerhouse: the Hudson's Bay Company.

In 1832, Captain Benjamin L. E. Bonneville, a thirty-seven-year-old French-born West Point graduate, reached Nez Percé lands. He had served in the army in New England, Arkansas, Mississippi, and Missouri before taking leave to explore the West, intending to assess the strengths and weaknesses of Indian tribes and determine the potential for American trade and settlement. He led the first wagons west of the Continental Divide, following an Indian and game trail similar to the return route Astor's overland party had used in 1812.

Bonneville crossed the Divide at South Pass, a wide

sagebrush-covered opening in the mountains in central Wyoming, and met a party of Nez Percés on the Upper Salmon River in Idaho. He asked the Indians to join his party in a hunt, but they declined, according to Warren Angus Ferris, a trapper traveling with Bonneville, because "it was a sacred day to them, and the Great Spirit would be angry should they devote it to hunting." In a later encounter, Bonneville castigated the Nez Percés for not retaliating against the Blackfeet who had raided them. "Unless you rouse yourselves from your apathy and strike some bold and decisive blow," he lectured, "you will cease to be considered men, or objects of manly warfare." A Nez Percé spokesman replied that they did not seek revenge because they had "a heart for peace, not for war."

Bonneville entered the Nez Percé homeland, the Wallowa Valley of northeastern Oregon, a year later and invited the Wallowa Band to begin trading furs with the Americans. The Indians, however, were reluctant to break their ties with the Hudson's Bay Company.

The Indians of the Columbia Basin first came into contact with Christian missionaries in 1825 when the chiefs of the Kutenai and Spokan tribes each allowed a son to be taken to the Red River Mission in Canada, where they would be educated at a missionary school. The boys, given the names J. H. Pelly and Nicholas Garry but better known as Kutenai Pelly and Spokan Garry, learned to read and write, studied geography and how to cultivate and harvest crops, and, of course learned about the white man's religion. When they returned to their homes with a Hudson's Bay Company expedition in 1829, they carried with them leather-bound copies of the

King James Bible, a New Testament, and the Church of England's Book of Common Prayer. Once reunited with their own people, they talked about the men of God. Spokan Garry, whose father had died while he was at Red River, rose to prominence as he traveled through the Columbia River Basin telling the tribes about Jesus, the Ten Commandments, and the concepts of hell and heaven. Because he often read from his Bible and used it during his preaching, the Cayuse, Nez Percé, and Flathead tribes* who lived there soon considered the book to have a supernatural message. For them status depended on power, which could be obtained by success on the battlefield or in hunting. Power also came from the spirit world, so the message Spokan Garry shared seemed a direct link.

In the spring of 1830, the Hudson's Bay Company took five more young boys to the Red River mission for instruction. Among them were two Nez Percés, Ellice, the grandson of powerful war chief Red Grizzly Bear, who had met Lewis and Clark, and another boy. Significantly, the nephew of Cayuse leader Young Chief also made his way to Red River. This boy was related to the Nez Percés, as his father was a half brother to the Wallowa Band member who became Joseph's father. Sending this boy to the mission brought status to Young Chief and may explain in part why Joseph's father later became one of the first Nez Percé converts to Christianity.

The Nez Percés were not content to watch other tribes

---

*All three tribes got their common names from trappers, the Cayuses for horses, the Nez Percés for ornaments a few early people wore in their noses, and the Flatheads for their early-day practice of shaping infant heads with cradleboards.

make connection—and therefore gain influence—with the powerful book and the message that the men of God could bring to them and so decided to take the initiative. Four tribesmen left their secure villages in 1831, traveling with some Flathead allies over mountains, across desert-like lands, and along rivers, making a two-thousand-mile journey through unknown territory to ask for their own religious teachers. In St. Louis they found assistance from an old ally, William Clark, then Superintendent of Indian Affairs for Louisiana Territory.

Although Clark assisted them, St. Louis took its toll. Two of the Nez Percés developed fevers and died in the city. A third died en route home of "disease which he had contracted in the civilized district"; so wrote the artist George Catlin, who had painted a portrait of the man just days before his death.

The fourth Nez Percé emissary, Rabbit Skin Leggings, accompanied fur traders back to the West in 1832, arriving in time for the trappers' trade fair, called rendezvous, in Pierre's Hole, southwest of Yellowstone National Park. After the rendezvous he joined a party of Nez Percés as they moved north to hunt buffalo. During evenings in camp Rabbit Skin Leggings told his new companions about his adventures in St. Louis. In March 1833, his buffalo-hunting band engaged in a fight with enemy Blackfeet and he was killed. His companions carried stories of Rabbit Skin's journey to the Nez Percé lodges, sharing them during storytelling sessions in winter camp.

All this happened before the birth of the child who would become Chief Joseph.

To understand Joseph as boy and man requires understanding a lasting influence on his life, the Christian missionaries who ventured out to Nez Percé country with a single "mission": to tear the Indians from their ancient beliefs, "civilize" them, and make them farmers rather than hunters and gatherers. The first Christian to reach their homelands was the Reverend Samuel Parker, who along with Dr. Marcus Whitman rode horses from the Missouri River to the 1835 rendezvous held on the Green River in northwestern Wyoming. Parker, a fifty-six-year-old Congregational minister and former Ithaca, New York, teacher, could be arrogant, but he also respected Indians and believed they were the equals of white people. Whitman, from Wheeler, New York, was thirty-three, an unmarried, hardworking, and dedicated Presbyterian missionary-physician.

To travel west the two men joined a fur company brigade as it brought supplies to the annual trapper rendezvous. After learning of the desire for more missionaries in Oregon, Washington, Idaho, and western Montana, Whitman returned east with the fur brigade, while Parker, aged and ailing, continued on with a party of Nez Percés to find suitable locations for the missions. They took a route following the Continental Divide north, then struck west across central Idaho on a trail the Indians had followed on hunting and trading expeditions for generations.

While with the Nez Percés, Parker wrote in his journal that the people were "truly dignified and respectable in their manners and general appearance . . . cheerful and often gay, sociable, kind and affectionate . . . kind to strangers, and remarkably so to each other . . . scrupulously honest in all their dealings, and lying is scarcely known. They say they fear to sin against the Great Spirit, and therefore, they have but one heart, and their tongue is straight and not forked."

At that early date, when few whites had ventured even close to the Nez Percé homeland, Parker made a surprising notation in his journal saying "learned diplomats" would need to deal with the "deep and intricate questions" related to land ownership. He wrote that "my private opinion [is] that the Indians have a priority of claim." He also spoke of the Nez Percé leadership and society: "Probably there is no government upon earth where there is so much personal and political freedom, and at the same time so little anarchy." He added: "I can unhesitatingly say, that I have no where witnessed so much subordination, peace, and friendship as among the Indians in the Oregon Territory. The day may be rued when their order and harmony shall be interrupted by any instrumentality whatever."

While Samuel Parker was getting his first taste of Nez Percé life, Dr. Marcus Whitman returned to New York. There he recruited other missionaries to head west, married twenty-seven-year-old New Yorker Narcissa Prentiss, a judge's daughter who had herself been accepted into the missionary field, and arranged for supplies and transportation back to the West. In the spring of 1836, the Whitmans were joined by a frail Eliza Spalding, who rode in a Dearborn wagon and on her own sidesaddle accompanying Henry, her Presbyterian missionary husband, to what would become their own missions, the first established within the Nez Percé and Cayuse nations.

The Whitmans and Spaldings, traveling with fellow missionary William Gray, a twenty-six-year-old cabinetmaker the mission board had appointed to serve as a mechanic and helper, accompanied a fur trade caravan to rendezvous. Afterward, with Nez Percé guides, they brought their wagon over the Bear River Divide, along the Wyoming and Idaho boundary, making steep ascents and harrowing descents on a route no wagon had ever traveled. At Fort Hall, the Hudson's Bay post that trader Nathaniel Wyeth had established in 1834 on the Portneuf River of southeastern Idaho, Whitman modified the wagon into a two-wheeled cart. From this point, Eliza Spalding and Narcissa Whitman rode their sidesaddle horses to the mission sites Parker had chosen for them.

The Whitmans established themselves at Waiilatpu—the Place of the Rye Grass—to serve the Cayuses whose territory lay north and west of Nez Percé lands. Henry and Eliza Spalding turned back to the east, eventually following the Clearwater River to its confluence with Lapwai Creek. There they established a mission they called Lapwai, known to the Indians as the Place of the Butterflies. It lay up the stream in the heart of Nez Percé country at a site long used as a tribal winter camp. There were few living trees at the site, but ample wood for heating and cooking from the hundreds of trees washed down the river each spring and that piled up on the riverbank where the stream curved, widened, and slowed.

The Nez Percés, who had long hoped men of God would venture to their country, believing the Christians had great power that they would share with the People, helped erect the first mission buildings for the Spaldings. They cut logs in forests miles away, hauled them by hand to the mission site, and stacked them into walls. They gathered rocks and mortared them into fireplaces in new buildings, built a sawmill and a gristmill, and broke soil for gardens. They began attending church services, and when Eliza opened schoolbooks adults came to learn, bringing their children with them.

One of the first Nez Percé converts to Christianity was the Wallowa headman Tuekakas. He was rechristened Joseph and eventually Spalding gave him a New Testament version of the Book of Matthew written in the Nez Percé language. The book became one of Joseph's most prized possessions, one that he treasured for many years before he realized that the whites had certain ideas about his people's lands that troubled him.

In those disturbing years, Old Joseph, as Tuekakas became known, had the present and future of his people in his mind as he watched the Spaldings at their Christianizing work and later saw Marcus Whitman leading the first white-topped wagons through the country. "I was a boy then," Old Joseph's son later said, "but I remember well my father's caution. He had sharper eyes than the rest of our people."

They Were Like Grizzly Bears

The infant's lusty cry tore through the smoky darkness of the cave on a steep hillside in the heart of the Wallowa, and with that piercing wail Old Joseph had another son, a boy to teach and train in the ways of the People. In years to come that child became Hin-mah-too-yah-lat-kekt, Thunder Traveling to Loftier Mountain Heights.* When he was a baby he was baptized Ephraim by Reverend Henry Spalding, but white settlers would give him his father's name, Joseph.

The baby, his face almost square in its proportions and set off by a thick mat of black hair, peered up at his father with piercing dark eyes. This place of his birth, above a stream to

---

*There are various interpretations and spellings for Joseph's Nez Percé name, and for other Indian names as well; I use the most commonly accepted forms, relying, primarily, on interpretations in *Yellow Wolf*, by L. V. McWhorter. Throughout Joseph's life, fellow tribesmen referred to him only by his native name.

become known as Joseph Creek, for the father and most particularly for the son, became one of the younger Joseph's favored camping places and had also been the place where his grandmother had lived and died. It was ground that nurtured him from the time he was a baby strapped in a cradleboard upon his mother's back as she dug kouse and camas roots or tended the fires used to preserve the salmon harvested from the free-flowing rivers. Located high in the Wallowa Valley, the ancestral homeland of his band, the area was sacred to his family and fellow tribesmen, a place where he would grow strong and learn the skills of his father, particularly as orator and leader. It was a place to seek his *Wyakin*, or spirit helper. Within this circle of Nez Percé homeland, he would live and die as had the people of the tribe who came before him.

In 1840, the summer of Joseph's birth, the first emigrant family made its way to Oregon, harbinger of a flood of pioneers seeking free, fertile land in the West. The next year, two dozen emigrants brought covered wagons drawn by oxen and mules to Fort Hall in Idaho. These pioneers abandoned their wagons and found Nez Percé guides who led them on foot and horseback to the Waiilatpu Mission in Washington near the Walla Walla River.

Joseph had other brothers and sisters, but the one closest to him throughout his life was Ollokot, or Frog, born in 1843. Both boys took their names from uncles, as was common among their people, Joseph from his mother's Nez Percé brother and Ollokot from his father's Cayuse half brother.

Ollokot had a stoutness of heart and sharpness of mind that he would demonstrate many years later as the war leader for this band of Nez Percés. Together these two sons were the future of the Wallowa Band and the entire Nez Percé nation.

By age three, Joseph toddled around camp pretending with other little boys that he was a great warrior or hunter. Already he had been taught the importance of ritual cleanliness. Each day from the time he was a baby, he had been bathed in icy streams or warm waters if they were available, a practice he would continue, along with sweat baths, throughout his life. He now rode his own horse, and when the tribe moved from one campsite to another his mother or father would put him on a Nez Percé woman's saddle, which had a high front and back pommel and cantle, tying him in place should he become sleepy. In the tribal tradition, a young child would spend much time with grandparents, the primary teachers of important lessons. In Joseph's case, since there was no grandfather to fulfill that duty, he learned from his father and uncles.

For Joseph and Ollokot, days and years were marked by the rituals of the tribe. At age three or four they began fishing for salmon, learning the net and spear as the salmon jumped and slithered and struggled upstream fighting the current and the rock-strewn river bottoms. They saw their father and other men gamble and engage in stick games where they guessed how many sticks someone held in a hidden hand. While the boys played with toy bows and arrows, their mother and the older girls and women used pointed fire-hardened sticks with antler handles to dig the camas bulbs from the ground on the Weippe Prairie and at Camas Prairie or near Tolo Lake north of the Salmon River in Idaho. After the freshly harvested plant dried, the women rubbed away the black outer coat to expose the white bulb. They dug a small pit in the ground, lined it with heated stones, covered the rocks with dirt, placed the bulbs in a circular pile in the pit, and covered them with a layer of grass. The cooks poured water over the grass to create steam when it hit the hot rocks below, then added another layer of dirt and built a fire on top of the mound, keeping it burning overnight or longer. After the fire burned down, the women uncovered the roasted camas roots, which were then sweet and edible. To further preserve the roots, the women pounded them between stones to create a dough that was then rolled in grass and shaped into heavy cakes. Once again the cooks prepared a roasting pit and, following additional baking, separated the large cakes into smaller portions about a half inch thick to be dried in the sun or placed over a smoky fire. Once prepared in this manner, camas would last for months. Joseph and his family had plenty to eat in their land of great bounty, but even so, his mother and the other women always cached food for use in lean times.

Summer found the family traveling from one harvesting site to another gathering a variety of plant foods: wild potato that they boiled and peeled; kouse, a root that could be cooked or eaten raw and which had a flavor that provided its name: biscuit root; wild carrot, dug in June or July; and yampa, another carroty-tasting bulb they cooked or ate raw. Joseph's mother traded for bitterroot from Indian women in Montana, boiling these to reduce their acrid taste before seasoning them with fat and wild fruits such as huckleberries, serviceberries, blackberries, and chokecherries. On such harvesting journeys, Joseph and Ollokot helped herd the horses of their band as soon as they were old enough to control their own mounts. In winter they congregated in the tule-mat-covered village longhouses that stretched forty or more feet long and had multiple fires to gather around and listen to the storytelling of their elders, learning the history of their people and what was expected of them as young Nez Percé men.

Until he was seven years old, Joseph and his family spent much time camped near the Spalding Mission at Lapwai, where his father attended classes taught by Eliza Spalding and where he and Ollokot also sat in the schoolroom for a time, learning to read and to speak some English.

As they grew beyond childhood, the young people of the tribe ventured off by themselves, finding high mountain sites where they could seek a *Wyakin*, or guardian spirit helper, knowing such a helper would provide strength, courage, and skill. This custom might not have been followed by Joseph had his father retained his close ties to the Reverend Spalding, but by the time the child was seven his father had pulled away from the mission, rejecting many of the Christian teachings and returning to the traditions of his people.

When he was between ten and twelve years old, Joseph sought to find his *Wyakin*. After instruction from elders, he left the village, taking no food or water, and made his way to a high rocky ledge where he settled upon a bed of pine boughs and prepared himself mentally as he awaited a vision. Though the experiences he had on his quest would remain forever locked in his heart, by the time he returned to his village he had indeed received a spirit helper who gave him a song and power related to thunder. At the time he received it, a Nez Percé might not understand his spirit song, but as he grew older its meaning would become clear to him; later he would sing it in the longhouse during tribal Winter Guardian Spirit Dances and at other times when he needed the power attached to the song.

As had been done for generations, young Nez Percé men and older boys made a long journey over the Lolo Pass in the northern Bitterroot Mountains by following the Lochsa River to the Continental Divide and then crossing to the buffalo country in Montana. They took the old game and Indian trail, the same route Lewis and Clark followed on their own journeys over the Bitterroots in 1805 and 1806. Sometimes the Indians took the Southern Nez Percé Trail, the route Samuel Parker had crossed in 1835 and one that had been used for decades by the Nez Percés traveling to the fur rendezvous or other trading fairs. Some buffalo-hunting trips lasted two years, giving young boys experience in both hunting and fighting, for enemies lived in country beyond their homeland. The Nez Percés forged alliances with some of the tribes to the east, particularly the Flatheads in the northern Bitterroot country and the Crows, who made their home along the Yellowstone River, the heart of the buffalo grounds.

While his younger brother Ollokot made several journeys, giving him much experience in hunting and fighting and leading to his eventual position as the war leader of the Wallowa Band, Joseph made only one trip to the buffalo country, no doubt as the rite of passage common among Nez Percé boys. Even as a teenager Joseph had responsibilities to the band that he would eventually lead. Instead of venturing to the buffalo range, he sat in council listening to the headmen and consulting with his father and other elders, who taught him the ways of the People and gave him the grounding to administer discipline as well as compassion. "I carried a heavy load upon my back ever since I was a boy," he would one day lament.

Great changes were unfolding in the Nez Percé homelands, initiated by the missionaries who encouraged Indian men to farm and harvest crops. Traditionally women harvested the food and prepared or preserved it for use, while the men hunted and all tribal members fished. But, from the time of Samuel Parker's first summer with the Nez Percés in 1835, men were taught to plow the earth and plant crops and the missionaries even urged them to help the women with camp chores, such as setting up lodges when the tribe moved. Older Nez Percés believed such work degraded the men.

Perhaps it was the strife so evident among the missionaries themselves that led to the division among the Nez Percé people. The Whitmans and Spaldings had sparred even as they made their way overland in 1836 and continued in conflict in succeeding years. Spalding governed his Lapwai mission with a firm hand, one that often held a lash, administering whippings to the Indians he ministered to and even forcing tribal members to wield a strap against their own people, all the while preaching moving sermons that led the Indians to pledge their lives to the Christian God.

Besides the occasional—and sometimes vitriolic—disagreements between the Whitmans and Spaldings, there was other religious discord. In the years after the first two missions opened, more churchmen and -women came to the region, representing both Protestant and Catholic faiths. Then, too, William Gray, who had traveled west in 1836 with the Whitman-Spalding party, remained in the area, continually creating problems. In one incident, he convinced Nez Percé tribesmen to provide him with horses that he would take back east and trade for cattle. But before he could exchange the horses, two Nez Percés who accompanied him returned to their tribal home and a third died in an attack on Gray's party by enemy Lakota Indians. When the two Nez Percés who had traveled with Gray returned home with their horses instead of cattle, Spalding furiously ordered them whipped. One of the Indians took his horses and rode back to his village near Kamiah, but the other remained at the mission. There the order for the flogging became the subject of a serious clash between Spalding and the Nez Percés, who refused to administer it. Eventually Spalding did the thrashing, with the result of a loss of his prestige among the Indians of the region.

Spalding sparred with other missionaries over control of the Clearwater bands of Nez Percé; Whitman had escalating difficulties with the Cayuses, whose headmen, Five Crows and Young Chief, were Old Joseph's half brothers. Surprisingly, frail Eliza Spalding developed the best relationship with the Indians. They came to her school for instruction, sitting quietly and attentively. But for her husband the situation was much different. When her health failed and she was unable to continue, he took over teaching and attendance quickly spiraled downward. At their mission, headman Big Thunder used his influence among members of other Nez Percé bands to urge them to leave the mission and return to their homelands.

Although he had been an early and devout convert, by the

late 1840s Old Joseph no longer had faith in Henry Spalding's religious teachings. He and others rejected Christian beliefs and returned to their own customs. He embraced the beliefs and teachings of Smohalla, a Wanapam* medicine man from the Priest River country of Oregon. Smohalla based his message on experiences he had during a sacred vision quest, telling his followers that they should again rely on visions and dreams. If they did, he said, Indians who had died would return to life and cause the white men to disappear. His teachings were similar to those of other Indian prophets, including those in the times of Pontiac and Tecumseh, who had rallied varied tribes and who were to do so again in the Ghost Dance message of Wovoka delivered to the Plains Indians in the 1880s.

Smohalla's message struck home with some Nez Percés, who became known as Dreamers, and their path began to diverge from their Christian brethren who believed in and supported the message of the missionaries.

One day the division between Christian Nez Percés and Dreamers would extend beyond religion.

White emigrants followed the missionaries, bringing additional change to Nez Percé country. The 875 emigrants traveling what became the Oregon Trail in 1843 jumped to 1,475 in 1844 and 2,500 in 1845. The numbers declined in 1846, in part due to unrest created by the Mexican-American War, but in 1847 the floodgates to the West reopened and some four thousand people walked and drove wagons to the Oregon

---

*This tribal name means "river people," for their territory along the Columbia River.

country. Most emigrants bypassed Nez Percé lands, particularly that of the Wallowa Band, closest to the trail but isolated
by steep mountains.

Many early migrants made their way to the Whitman mission, usually stopping for a short time to rest and "recruit," or
prepare for the final leg of the overland and river journey to
the Willamette farmlands farther west. Migration provided
some benefits to the Wallowa and other Nez Percés, who
found they could trade for worn-out cattle. These animals,
given an opportunity to graze on lush high country grasses
would recover and become a long-standing food source and
form of wealth and prestige for the people. But the overland
travelers brought misery with them, too, particularly to the
Cayuses, whose territory was north and west of the Nez Percé
country.

Measles, a disease fatal to the Indians, arrived with the
great influx of emigrants in 1847, and Marcus Whitman
found his resources and abilities taxed to the limit as he
treated the victims. Most of the pioneers and their children
survived, but the Indians lacked natural immunity to the disease, so, even with treatment, almost half the Cayuse tribe
died. The survivors became convinced that Whitman was not
caring for the stricken Indians properly, believed the encroaching emigrants wanted Cayuse land, and suspected that
Whitman and Spalding were poisoning their people. In
Cayuse culture, like that of the Nez Percés, if a medicine man
failed to heal and a tribesman died, relatives were permitted to
kill the healer. Thus, on November 29, 1847, the Cayuses attacked the Waiilatpu Mission, murdered Marcus and Narcissa
Whitman and nine others, and took many mission residents,
including women and children, captive. Henry Spalding had

been with Whitman just hours before the attack. The frenzied Indians sought to kill him, too, but with a warning from a Catholic priest he escaped his pursuers. Meantime, friendly Nez Percés warned Eliza Spalding of the attack and helped her and two of her children find refuge at the home of a former mountain man and his Nez Percé wife.

Due to their proximity and kinship ties, the Wallowa Band of Nez Percés faced stiff pressure to join the Cayuse uprising, but Old Joseph refused to aid his half brothers, Young Chief and Five Crows, who had been wounded after the initial attack at Waiilatpu. Instead Old Joseph announced to soldiers who had responded to the crisis, "When I left my home I took the book [his copy of the Book of Matthew] in my hand and brought it with me. It is my light. . . . I speak for all the Cayuses present, and all my people. I do not want my children engaged in this war, although my brother is wounded. You speak of the murderers [of those at the Whitman mission]. I shall not meddle with them. I bow my head. This much I speak."

Following his statement, which carried much weight because of his blood relationship to both the Nez Percé and Cayuse people, other important headmen from his tribe also refused to align with the Cayuses. As they had done when Lewis and Clark first entered their lands, Joseph's tribe maintained a peaceful interaction with the Americans.

By the time Nathaniel Wyeth of the Hudson's Bay Company negotiated the ransom of the captives taken by the Cayuses, the end had been written for Waiilatpu. While their situation became tense, if not deadly, Henry and Eliza Spalding departed their mission for a final time after being reunited with their eldest daughter who had been present during the attack on Waiilatpu. Eliza never came back—she died in 1851—but Henry returned to the Nez Percé country many years later.

The violent end of the Whitman mission caused whites in the region to demand federal control and on August 14, 1848, led to the establishment of Oregon Territory by Congress, a vast region that then included most of the lands west of the Continental Divide and north of Nevada and California.

Emigrant travel to Oregon resumed after the California Gold Rush of 1849, peaking in 1852 when ten thousand people made their way overland. By then the Nez Percés began to feel genuinely threatened by the white wave. As Joseph later said, "We were like deer. They were like grizzly bears."

I Have Bought Your Horses

In 1802, Senator John Quincy Adams of Massachusetts wrote that "the Indian right of possession itself stands, with regard to the greatest part of the country, upon a questionable foundation" and raised questions with his senatorial colleagues about Indian control of extensive forest and agricultural lands. "Shall the exuberant bosom of the common mother, amply adequate to the nourishment of millions, be claimed exclusively by a few hundreds of her offspring?" he asked.

When Thomas Jefferson negotiated with France in 1803 to purchase the Louisiana Territory, thereby doubling the physical landmass of the United States, he outlined what would become Indian policy over the next several decades. Indians had land that the growing nation wanted. Because the tribesmen sought trade goods, Jefferson suggested the way to force expansion was to "see the good and influential among them in debt, because we observe that when these debts get beyond what the individuals can pay, they become willing to lop them off by a cession of lands."

By the late 1830s federal Indian policy, guided through political channels by President Andrew Jackson, had pushed the Delawares out of their northeastern forestlands and removed the Cherokees, Choctaws, Chickasaws, Seminoles, and Creeks from their homes in the Southeastern United States to the Southern Plains, then known as Indian Territory.* Over the next forty years even more tribes would find themselves removed to that Indian Territory or forced onto remote, ever-shrinking reservations.

At age fifteen Joseph rode with his father to a council organized by Joel Palmer, Oregon's Superintendent of Indian Affairs, and Washington Territory's Governor and Superintendent of Indian Affairs, Isaac I. Stevens. There, near the Walla Walla River, Joseph saw the first erosion of Nez Percé country and sovereign rule. "After the council was opened," he would say many years later, Governor Stevens "made known his heart. He said there were a great many white people in the country, and many more would come."

On May 21, 1855, Stevens and Palmer reached the council grounds, where they found two pole arbors covered with tree boughs that advance workers had constructed. One arbor would be used for negotiations, and the Indians could gather and eat under the other. The workers also built a log storehouse, filled it with gifts for the Indians, and erected tents to

---

*Indian Territory encompassed most of the current state of Oklahoma.

serve as quarters and mess area for government negotiators and their assistants.

Three days later the two Indian superintendents watched in awe as 2,500 Nez Percés came in like centaurs. Carrying an American flag, the men had on battle attire: leather and cloth breechclouts, beaded moccasins, feathers in their hair, and jewelry including multiple loop necklaces made from shells and beads. Red, yellow, and white paint decorated their faces and their horses' rumps, legs, and around their eyes. The headmen wore feathered bonnets and the warriors feathers in their hair. Even the horses of the lead men had feather headstalls placed over their forelocks. Following their headmen, a thousand men galloped by twos toward the American representatives. They brandished bows and arrows, held up their shields, banged on drums, and shot the few guns they had among them as they chanted, whooped, and later danced to the drumbeats that resounded across the camp and echoed from the rye grass–covered hills above the council site near the Walla Walla River.

Meantime, the women unpacked their own horses and set up the Indian camp a half mile from the arbor where the treaty talks would take place. They unloaded lodge poles, placed them in circular patterns, and enclosed them with buffalo hides and bark mats; dug fire pits where they could cook meals of game, salmon, and camas root bread. Infant cradleboards sat in shady places beside the lodges and little boys and girls ran and played—this would be their home until it was time to pack camp and move again. Young boys herded the tribe's horses out onto the hills, finding the best grass and watering spots for the hundreds of animals required to move the people to the council site.

Lawyer, an awkward man with a straight nose and ready smile who stood five feet, eight inches tall in his beaded moccasins, got his name for his oratorical skills and thus had been chosen by his cohorts as the chief spokesman for the combined Nez Percé bands. Other headman would add their voices, too, including Old Joseph, James, and Eagle-From-the-Light. Conspicuously absent was Looking Glass, the powerful seventy-year-old Nez Percé war chief whose homeland was in the Asotin region in southern Washington, for he was still hunting in the buffalo country. The Walla Walla, Cayuse, Yakima, Palouse, and Umatilla tribes had representatives on hand; Spokan Garry was present for his tribe.

Five days after riding to the council grounds, Joseph found a seat near the treaty arbor, watching and listening as his father and the other headmen began negotiating. During the three weeks that followed, Isaac Stevens, a politically ambitious thirty-five-year-old West Point graduate, outlined plans for three reservations to serve the Columbia Basin tribes. One encompassed three million acres along the north side of the Snake River, plus the Clearwater, Salmon, Grande Ronde, Wallowa, and Imnaha valleys to be used by the various Nez Percé bands. There would be separate tribal reservations for the Yakimas, Palouses, and Klikitats in the upper drainage of the Yakima River and for the Umatilla, Cayuse, and Walla Walla tribes along the Umatilla River in the Blue Mountains of Oregon. The Spokans would remain near the Spokane River in northern Washington.

The Indians did not meekly accede to efforts to pen them into smaller regions. At an earlier all–Nez Percé gathering, the headmen had agreed they would stand, define the boundaries of their individual territories, and demand that their lands be retained in full. Spokesmen for other tribes, however, did not have the power of the Nez Percés. While Stevens and Palmer outlined proposals that would restrict their territory, tension under the council arbor became palpable as Indian hands flexed, seeking weapons that had been left outside the council area. When whisperings of a plot by Cayuses against Stevens and his party spread across the camps, Lawyer placed his lodge near that of the white negotiator, giving notice that the numerous and mighty Nez Percés would side with the council organizers should trouble break out.

There were reports that Lawyer moved to Stevens's camp for his own safety after many of his Nez Percé comrades hardened their stance against him and the conciliatory message he had begun to share with the American treaty makers. However it occurred, Lawyer's move to Stevens's camp again placed Nez Percé leadership in a position of loyalty to the Americans.

The discussions spread over weeks as translators defined proposals and responses. The headmen seated on the ground in a semi-circle beneath the arbor smoked and talked with Stevens and Palmer, who occupied a bench in front of them. A thousand Indians sat behind their leaders silently listening to the debate and understanding only portions of the negotiations. Most spoke only their native languages, though some understood a little English and many could follow the discussion if speakers used Chinook Jargon, a pidgin trade language with few words and simple grammar that was commonly used in the Pacific Northwest. Still, the speeches had to be translated into several different forms, making the treaty discussions time-consuming and tedious. A few Nez Percés, English trained at mission schools, recorded the proceedings in small notebooks.

"I think you intend to win our country," the Walla Walla headman Yellow Serpent told the white men. "In one day the Americans become as numerous as the grass. . . . Suppose you show me goods, shall I run up and take them? That is the way with all of us Indians as you know. Goods and the heart are not equal. Goods are for using on the earth."

To the Indians the earth represented their mother. As the Cayuse Steachus (also called Stickus) explained, "My friends, I wish to show you my heart. If your mother were in this country, gave you birth and suckled you, and while you were suckling, some person came and took away your mother and left you alone and sold your mother, how would you then feel? This is our mother—this country—as if we drew living from her."

This was, perhaps, the first time the Americans had heard this connection between the Indian people of the Columbia Basin with the earth as their mother. It would not be the last.

Palmer said the treaty would protect the Indians from those he called "bad white men" who were scheming "to get your horses." He knew that Stevens, who was the survey leader for a northern route across the country, clearly wanted the Indian land cessions to aid the railroad development. The two negotiators kept that fact quiet during the treaty discussions, instead allowing the tribal representatives to believe other whites threatened their lands and supporting the premise that a treaty would protect Indian homelands.

When not negotiating with the Americans, the Indians held footraces and horse races, Nez Percés pitting their superior animals against one another and the horses of the other tribes. These were friendly contests staged during leisure time, but the Nez Percé speeches in council had begun to drive a wedge between their tribe and others from the region. As Old

Joseph's Cayuse half brother Five Crows put it, "Listen to me, you chiefs. We have been as one people with the Nez Percés heretofore. This day we are divided." One evening, as the leaders of all tribes except the Nez Percés sat up late, smoking and arguing over the proposals that had been made, Lieutenant Lawrence Kip, a New Yorker and former student at West Point who served as a staff officer at the council, made his way from Indian camp to Indian camp and reported, "The Cayuse and other tribes were very much incensed against the Nez Percés."

Just when it looked like an agreement had been reached to establish the reservation boundary, Nez Percé solidarity itself became threatened by Looking Glass's return from his buffalo hunting trip. Dressed in war attire, his forehead painted red for battle, and carrying a staff with a fresh Blackfeet scalp on it, he stormed into the council and demanded, "My people, what have you done? While I am gone, you have sold my country. I have come home, and there is not left me a place to pitch my lodge. Go home to your lodges. I will talk with you."

Looking Glass then turned his attention to Stevens and Palmer, demanding more land for the Nez Percés. In response, Lawyer stomped out of the council, but the other tribal headmen remained. Wrangling continued among the factions until finally the Nez Percé headmen agreed to terms and made their marks on the treaty. By standing together, the Nez Percés retained a region of nearly five thousand square miles and would receive $60,000 in "improvements" plus another $200,000 in annuities—goods such as clothing and food—for their people. They had bargained from a position of strength and held on to most of their tribal lands in Idaho and Oregon, giving up only border areas. Old Joseph, satisfied that he still controlled the Wallowa Valley, scrawled an awkward *X* on the parchment beside his name and just below the marks of Lawyer and Looking Glass. Despite the latter's protests, the Nez Percé chiefs believed they had a good treaty. Such was not the case for the Umatillas, Walla Wallas, Cayuses, and other tribes at the council, who would see their homelands dissipate almost as the ink dried upon the document.

Once returned to Wallowa Valley, Old Joseph found a piece of parchment sixteen inches wide by eighteen inches long that he used to draw a map of his territory. On it he placed the principal rivers: the Imnaha, the Wallowa, the Snake, and the Grande Ronde. He added the beautiful Wallowa Lake, the rugged peaks of the Wallowa Range of the Blue Mountains, and the high plateau and canyon lands where his wives harvested camas and kouse, where his sons Joseph and Ollokot fished for salmon or hunted for mountain sheep, elk, and deer, and where he ran horses and cattle. Perhaps for a time the old headman truly believed his *X* on a government treaty and a hand-drawn parchment map would preserve the sanctity of his homeland for his people.

Because of erroneous press reports orchestrated by Isaac Stevens and Joel Palmer just days after the treaty signing at Walla Walla, a number of whites moved into the region almost immediately, staking claims to land they had no right to even cross. "By an express provision of the treaty the country embraced in these cessions and not included in the reservation is open to settlement, excepting that the Indians are secured in the possession of their buildings and implements until removal to the reservation," Stevens and Palmer had reported in late June 1855 editions of newspapers in Oregon and Washington. The statement was not true and would not be for another four years, but as expected, settlers quickly came to the Columbia Basin, choosing acreage for farms and homes and staking the first gold claims on the Indian lands. A few turned back when they met Indians positioned at mountain passes telling them not to trespass into their treaty lands; others ignored the warnings, in some cases with deadly consequences.

In 1859, the United States Senate ratified the treaty negotiated at Walla Walla four years earlier. The tribes received no payments or annuities during those intervening years and there had been no progress on the promises of the negotiators for schools, sawmills, blacksmith, carpentry and wagon shops, and gristmills. The first payments and annuity gifts came in 1860, but Old Joseph and other headmen, including Looking Glass, refused to accept them since, by then, there had been significant changes within the Nez Percé tribe: Christian Nez Percés and the Dreamers were taking diverging trails. Like his father, Joseph followed the Dreamer practices, allowing his straight black hair to grow long so he could let it hang free or twist it into double braids that hung forward over his shoulders, sometimes wrapping them in fur pieces; he also cut a pompadour, greased it to stand upright, or rolled it back from his face.

In 1861, the Nez Percé headmen sought a new council to discuss the white encroachment onto their lands and the conflict such intrusion brought. Tension was rising, but governmental leaders failed to listen to the concerns and the Nez

Percés suffered both direct and indirect attacks. In June 1862, white miners killed three Indians in the Salmon River country with no consequences to the murderers.

Idaho newspapers reported on conflicts between miners and Indians and often stirred sentiment against the Nez Percés. In December 1865, when Indians attacked a Butterfield Overland Stage and Express coach, the *Owyhee Avalanche* editor in Silver City, Idaho, wrote: "[S]end some more blankets." Although not specifically stated, the suggestion for blankets implied a simple act of genocide as one way to deal with recalcitrant Indians. This offhand proposal of mass murder, not unusual in the Indian-hating frontier press of the era, even had a historic, though accidental, underpinning: white traders had introduced smallpox to the Indians of the Upper Missouri River in 1837. A deckhand on a traders' steamboat first contracted the disease and later infected three Arikara women, but the smallpox began its rampant sweep through the Upper Missouri tribes when they received infected blankets and cloth from the traders as part of their regular government annuities. Before running its course on the Upper Missouri, smallpox killed virtually all of the Mandans, half of the Arikara tribe, nearly half of the Blackfeet Confederation, and hundreds of Lakotas, Hidatsas, and Assiniboines. Although the epidemic of 1837 started accidentally, in 1763 defenders of Fort Pitt in Pennyslvania quelled an uprising of Delaware Indians when a Swiss mercenary at the fort intentionally gave Indian attackers two blankets and a handkerchief known to be infected with smallpox. The Nez Percés themselves had endured a smallpox epidemic in 1781–82 when the disease traveled across western Canada and spread to tribes in the Columbia Basin.

Although the Idaho settlers did not import smallpox-infested blankets to distribute among the Nez Percés, in February 1866 residents of Silver City offered a bounty on Indian scalps and formed a company of twenty-five volunteers to hunt Indians. The *Avalanche* outlined details of a town resolution that called for payments of $100 for a man's scalp, $50 for a woman's, and $25 "for everything in the shape of an Indian under ten years of age."

In partial response to Nez Percé objections to white encroachment, federal officials established Fort Lapwai in 1862 at a site south of Spalding's original mission. Construction of the military post brought the Nez Percé headmen to the area in November demanding a council, but the federal authorities refused to meet with the Indian leaders until mid-May 1863.

That same month, events in the War between the States were escalating in Virginia. Early in May one Union general who knew as little about the Nez Percés as they did of him but who, in a dozen years would become Joseph's nemesis was in a fight to hold his panicky troops in battle.

Newly promoted Major General Oliver Otis Howard implored the members of the Union Army's XI Corps to stand and fight as Confederate troops stormed their positions at Chancellorsville, Virginia, in early May 1863. He had been at his headquarters at Dowdall's Tavern on Plank Road near Chancellorsville earlier that afternoon. Upon hearing gunfire in the west, he mounted his horse, at first seeing scared deer and rabbits running from the frightening noise. Soon his own troops ran: all of the First Division came at him in "a terrible gale," as he later wrote.

Some of Howard's men tried to stop the race of their comrades away from the Confederate attack, and an aide suggested Howard should himself begin firing not at the enemy but at his own men in order to stem the flow. The pious general could do no such thing. Instead he shocked the fleeing troops back into the fight by gripping a Union flag under the stump of the arm he'd lost after being shot twice in the May 1862 Battle of Fair Oaks, waving the banner while yelling at his men. In response, more than one Union fighter checked his flight, turned, and stood in defiance of the oncoming Confederates.

The men eventually put up a fight, but the Federals still lost the battle at Chancellorsville to the Confederates that day, in part due to the negligence of General Howard, who had not adequately protected his army's right flank. There would be more fighting later that month near Vicksburg, and in June and July Howard was at Gettysburg as the American nation further tore itself asunder.

By 1863 Joseph stood five feet, eleven inches tall and weighed more than 200 pounds. He was strong and handsome, wearing a mixture of Nez Percé garments including fringed or cloth leggings with cuffs, moccasins, and a warm coat made from a Hudson's Bay point blanket that sheltered him from wind and cold. Around his neck he wore multiple looped strands of white shell beads and a double choker made of variously colored beads. He parted his hair on the right side, twisting it into braids, and swept his pompadour up and to the left, sometimes coating it with a white powder to make it more prominent. Though he had learned to read and write some English when he sat at a desk in Eliza Spalding's mission school as a child, now he spoke only his native language or used Chinook Jargon to converse with surrounding tribes and whites. Already he was stepping in his father's tracks as spokesman for the Wallowa Band.

That year the Nez Percés finally gathered in council with the representatives of the United States government to try to work out an agreement that would halt the march of white settlers and miners onto their lands. The council document, which became known as the Thief Treaty, led to the permanent fracturing of Nez Percé power.

Twenty-three-year-old Joseph rode with his father, his twenty-year-old brother, Ollokot, and others from the Wallowa Band to the treaty grounds where they expected to make it clear that the whites on Nez Percé land needed to leave. Although no settlers or miners had yet encroached upon the isolated Wallowa Valley, Joseph and his companions supported the other Nez Percé bands where whites were building cabins and tearing the ground of the Earth Mother as they dug for gold. Other Dreamers joined them at the council: White Bird, Looking Glass, Eagle-From-the-Light, Big Thunder, and Toolhoolhoolzote, a respected medicine man and tribal leader, among them.

From the moment the council opened, the Dreamer Nez Percés faced trouble. Indian Superintendent Calvin H. Hale and Commissioners S. D. Howe and Charles Hutchins opened the parley by proposing a reduction in the Nez Percé reservation from 5,000 square miles to a space of only 500 square miles, a reduction that included all of the Wallowa Band's territory. In 1855, the Nez Percé chiefs would have walked off together in angry defiance had they heard such a drastic proposal, but by the opening of the new council Nez Percé solidarity had begun to weaken. Indian objection forced the commissioners to add $75,000 in goods such as food and clothing to the treaty proposal—yet there were undercurrents that would split the Nez Percé nation just as surely as the conflict over states' rights had launched the United States into civil war.

The fracture came because Lawyer, the headman who had been selected as the main spokesman for all the bands during the 1855 treaty council, and his tribal allies seemed to endorse government proposals. Those allies were primarily Christian Indians who already lived in the area the new reservation would include. Under the treaty, the non-Christian Dreamers would be required to abandon their regions and move to the reservation centered at Lapwai in Idaho.

Old Joseph and his allied headmen refused the terms: they could never sell their homelands, they said.

Lawyer initially stood with those who opposed further land cessions, telling Superintendent Hale, "Dig the gold, and look at the country, but we cannot give you the country you ask for." Other headmen made similar comments: "The boundary was fixed" under terms of the 1855 treaty, said one. "We understood that the whole of our reservation was for us, to cultivate and to occupy as we pleased. We cannot give up our country. . . . we cannot sell it to you."

The talks broke down, but neither the Indians nor the government negotiators left the council grounds. Instead, more Indians arrived each day, pitching their mat- and hide-covered lodges along the Lapwai Creek bottom, placing them close together in band groupings with space for women to congregate as they prepared food or socialized. The men rode their horses, ran races, and gambled. They played the stick game and participated in other contests of both luck and skill. Younger men, including Joseph, played flutes made from the branch of an elderberry tree as they courted women from other bands, seeking alliances that would forge new families and strengthen the tribe, since they did not marry within their own band, most often made up of siblings or cousins.

When negotiations resumed on June 3, 1863, the headmen had behind them some three thousand members of the Nez Percé nation. Agent S. D. Howe began the new talks by announcing to the Indians, "Many of your difficulties are caused by the extent of your Reservation, a few of you living at one place, and a few at another, so that you are scattered and divided." What he failed to recognize was that the physical separation of the various bands actually kept the nation intact by allowing individual bands—even individual Indians—personal freedom as had been noted by the Reverend Samuel Parker nearly thirty years earlier. Such isolation also kept volatile young men from organizing into powerful warrior groups bent on making trouble, while the practice of marrying outside their own band tied all the Nez Percés together into a larger tribe.

Unable to collectively bully the Indian leaders into signing a new treaty, the commissioners resorted to personal pressure. They adjourned the council and held private meetings with tribal headmen, starting with those who had indicated support for the government position, all of whom were Christian Nez Percés.

Upon resumption of the general council, the government representatives began pressing the anti-treaty band leaders, with Commissioner Hutchins telling them the Indians would be "as free as the Whites, to go where they pleased throughout the whole country, to hunt, to fish, to gather berries and dig cammas [*sic*]. They could take their horses and cattle, to graze them, on any lands outside, not in the occupancy of the whites."

Talks continued during the official council, but the real action occurred late into the night and early morning of June 4–5 when the Nez Percés gathered at their own council fire in the center of their extended village. The smoke of their pipes drifted around the council lodge and into the night air as the debate began. It still wafted hours later when Big Thunder "made a formal announcement of their determination to take no further part in the treaty," wrote eavesdropper and Oregon cavalry captain George Currey.

Currey and twenty Oregon cavalrymen rode to the council grounds about one o'clock in the morning of June 5. Upon seeing the fires still burning in the Nez Percé lodge, the captain and his troopers quietly moved closer, then watched and listened as the fifty-three Nez Percé headmen talked. After Big Thunder's first formal comment, Currey sat in shocked silence as the Indian headman, "in an emotional manner, declared the Nez Percé nation *dissolved*." The Dreamers from the anti-treaty faction and those supporting Lawyer and the pro-treaty Christian Nez Percés shook hands while Currey watched; then, he later wrote, Big Thunder announced "with a kind but firm demeanor that they would be friends, but a distinct people."

The powerful Nez Percé nation had just split apart, but unlike the American Union it would never be fully reunited.

"I withdrew my detachment," Currey wrote in his official

report, "having accomplished nothing but that of witnessing the extinguishment of the last council fires of the most powerful Indian nation on the sunset side of the Rocky Mountains."

Even before that landmark tribal council, Old Joseph and White Bird, the headman from the Salmon River country, had departed the council grounds; they refused to waste their breath attempting to reason with Lawyer. They did not agree with the treaty and by leaving would not be bound by it. In their culture a headman could negotiate only for his own band, not for people from another part of the tribe.

When the general council resumed on June 5, just three anti-treaty leaders remained: Big Thunder, Koolkool Snehee, and Eagle-From-the-Light. Hutchins quickly told them that when a "new arrangement" was made "the good Nez Percés will be wise, and rich and happy. You will be poor and miserable—and you will make your children poor and miserable." Then, with no knowledge of what the Nez Percés had done to their own nation during the night, he added, "If you persist in your disloyalty, we shall not regard you as Nez Percés, for the white men think that to be a Nez Percé means that you are good men."

Publicly in the treaty council the three remaining anti-treaty chiefs resisted governmental pressure, but privately, after assuring themselves that they would still have their traditional country on which to live, they agreed to the provisions. They did not, however, put their marks on the 1863 treaty, nor did any from the anti-treaty Dreamer faction. More significant, none of the signers were headmen who would have territory affected by the land cessions that the document required. Lawyer's name appeared first on the document, fol-

CHIEF JOSEPH

lowed by the other Christian Nez Percés, and with their signatures the Indian homeland was reduced to a tenth its original size and the unified Nez Percé nation ceased to exist.

The headmen who put their names or marks on the treaty
"sold all this land. Sold what did not belong to them," Joseph's
cousin Yellow Wolf later said.

Joseph put it another way: "Suppose a white man should
come to me and say, 'Joseph, I like your horses, and I want to
buy them.' I say to him, 'No, my horses suit me; I will not sell
them.' Then he goes to my neighbor and says to him, 'Joseph
has some good horses. I want to buy them, but he refuses to
sell.' My neighbor answers, 'Pay me the money, and I will sell
you Joseph's horses.' The white man returns to me and says,
'Joseph, I have bought your horses, and you must let me have
them.' *If we sold our lands to the government, this is the way they
were bought.*"

Joseph did not witness the breakup of his nation. With his father and other band members he mounted his horse and began the seventy-mile ride back to the Wallowa Valley before
that fateful tribal council started. His father did not sign the
Thief Treaty that took from the Nez Percés the Oregon valleys plus the canyon lands along the Salmon and Snake rivers
in Washington and Idaho, the region of the Upper Clearwater River, and the trails that crossed the Bitterroot Mountains
to the buffalo country of Montana. His heart heavy, Joseph
plunged his strong war horse into the churning Snake River,
fighting the fast current as he returned home. When Old
Joseph received a copy of the treaty, he ripped it into pieces
and then found his long-treasured copy of the Book of

Matthew and tore it apart as well, letting the words of the white man's God flutter across his beloved Wallowa Valley.

He did even more. "In order to have all people understand how much land we owned," Joseph later said, "my father planted poles around it." Piling rocks into cairns and placing ten-foot-high poles in them along a high ridge above Minam Creek on the western edge of the Wallowa Band lands, Old Joseph, like a mountain lion or a grizzly bear, marked his territory, telling his sons as they helped him, "Inside is the home of my people—the white man may take the land outside. Inside this boundary all our people were born. It circles the graves of our fathers, and we will never give up these graves to any man."

The rock cairns and pole markers placed by Old Joseph and his sons stood on the dividing ridge between the Grande Ronde and the Wallowa valleys. Because the ridge lay on the side of the valley where hundreds of Oregon Trail travelers had been passing since 1841, the tribesmen knew it was the direction from which the white settlers would come. While Old Joseph now realized a parchment map was not enough to exert his claim, his territorial markers became branded on his son's heart. Soon Joseph would assume his role as leader of this independent band, and he would fight with a ferocity his father could not even imagine.

I Have Spoken for My Country

S ome months after the treaty signing, Joseph rode to Lapwai to ask Whisk-tasket of the pro-treaty Nez Percés to be allowed to marry his daughter. Joseph had met the young woman when the bands congregated at the council. Nez Percé custom usually required an older woman from the groom's family to approach the bride-to-be's family, but Joseph, the clearly recognized heir-apparent to his powerful father, had options other young men did not have. A father must agree to the young man's suit, but Nez Percé weddings occurred only after the young couple spent time alone together as Joseph and He-yoom Yo-yikt (Bear Crossing), his bride-to-be, did following the 1863 council. They established compatibility and returned to her family to announce they would marry.

Both families gathered at Lapwai for the formal ceremony involving an exchange of gifts. Joseph's family gave horses and hunting and fishing gear, while the bride's people reciprocated with baskets, decorated and woven bags, digging sticks, and beads. After these formalities the families shared a meal of meat, roots, and breads. The relatives and tribal members acknowledged that Joseph and Bear Crossing were now officially married, and they departed to their home in the Wallowa Valley. By 1865, she had given birth to a daughter, Kapkap Ponmi (Sound of Running Water), who later took the name Sarah. Joseph would father three more daughters and five sons, none of whom lived to adulthood, and took three other wives, following the Nez Percé custom.

By 1867, after President Andrew Johnson ratified the 1863 treaty, Joseph had a new role. "My father became blind and feeble," he said. "He could no longer speak for his people. It was then I took my father's place as chief."

While assuming the mantle of headman for the Wallowas, he also cared for his own family. As Old Joseph's health failed—he could no longer ride alone but had a young boy mounted behind to help steady him in the saddle and handle the horse—Joseph and Ollokot spent much time with the old man. When they were small boys he had taught them the value of their people's traditions; now he seared into their souls a love for their homeland.

Within a year of its acceptance, the 1863 treaty called for the Wallowa Band to move to the reservation near Lapwai. President Johnson's ratification in 1867 reinforced that requirement. Even so, Joseph's people remained in their home country, periodically moving from winter campsites in Joseph Canyon or along the steep-sided Imnaha gorge to summer camps in the higher country of Oregon. In these places their thousands of cattle and horses could freely roam and graze on nutritious grasses or find shade under pine trees or beneath cottonwood and alder branches. Continuing their hunter-gatherer ways, the Wallowa Band routinely forded the powerful white-water currents of the Snake and Salmon rivers as they journeyed to the camas gathering grounds. They harvested salmon and the women collected wild fruit and berries to supplement their diet.

Old Joseph's message to his son to revere and hold on to the region continued as his strength ebbed: "You must stop your ears whenever you are asked to sign a treaty selling your home. A few years more and white men will be all around you. They have their eyes on this land."

The old man spoke the truth. By late 1864, settlers had cabins in the Grande Ronde Valley just west of the Wallowa and some of them eyed the lush pastureland to the east. Two years later William H. Odell made the first government survey in the Wallowa Valley, recording water, timber, and grazing lands. "I found many Indians camped upon the banks of the streams, taking great quantities of fish, while their large herds of horses grazed upon luxuriant grass," Odell wrote, predicting the homes of settlers would soon replace the "wigwam of the savage." Nez Percés resisted the intrusion. They pulled up Odell's survey stakes and scattered the rock monuments he had made. Even so, on May 28, 1867, a month after ratification of the 1863 treaty, the United States General Land Office officially included the Wallowa Valley in the public domain, thereby opening it to general settlement. The first white stockmen pushed cattle into the area in the spring of 1871, when two settlers, William McCormack and Neil

Keith, located homesteads on Hurricane Creek at the upper end of the valley and there built cabins and turned their cattle loose to fatten on the native bunchgrass.

A few months earlier, John B. Monteith became Indian Agent at Lapwai, appointed by President Ulysses S. Grant to implement his administration's "Peace Policy." The son of a Presbyterian minister, Monteith would eventually push both social and church reform on the Nez Percés, forcing them to surrender their old culture and religion.

Nez Percé horses grazed in the lush meadows along the Lostine River near Old Joseph's camp, a place settlers would soon know as Indian Town. A bluff rose behind the lodges, protecting the camp from late-summer breezes and causing smoke from individual campfires to rise lazily and disperse over the valley without smudging the clear blue sky. Inside one lodge Joseph leaned close to hear his father's whispered words. "My son, my body is returning to my Mother Earth," the weak, blind old man said. . . . "You are chief of these people. They look to you to guide them. . . ." A pause, the voice fading, rising, reminding: "White men . . . have their eyes on this land." Joseph, solemn in his father's final hours, nodded at the advice as he agreed to give the worldly goods the old chief owned to various relatives and friends. "Never sell the bones of your father and your mother," Old Joseph said. His sightless eyes bored into the young man, who pressed his father's hand a final time as he promised to protect the old man's grave with his life.

Word of Old Joseph's death spread quickly through the camp; women wailed their grief as friends and relatives prepared the body for burial. Joseph, now Chief Joseph, Ollokot, and other relatives led the way up the hill to the spot where they would lay the bones of the beloved leader, killing one of Old Joseph's horses to accompany him as he made his way to the spirit land. When the mourners returned to their camp, Joseph distributed robes, necklaces, tools, weapons, horses, and cattle to relatives and friends, making sure each person received what his father had willed. To complete the mourning cycle, tribesmen destroyed Old Joseph's sweat house, then those who had cared for the corpse purified themselves in their own ritual sweat house activities. In time they covered the grave with rocks and surrounded it with a rude fence before fastening a small bell on a pole above it as a symbol of their Dreamer beliefs. As the bell rang in the breeze, they believed the old man's spirit could begin its final journey.

Before his father's death Joseph had spoken for him in council with government agents; after burial he wore the title Chief Joseph with a dignity and solemnity that belied his age. At thirty-one, he was the youngest and least experienced of the Nez Percé leaders, but soon he would be catapulted onto a national stage all because of the power and pull of a piece of land. "There is nothing should supersede it. There is nothing which can outstrip it," he would say. "It is clothed with fruitfulness. In it are riches given me by my ancestors, and from that time up to the present I have loved the land, and was thankful that it had been given to me."

The season changed and he gathered his small band and headed into the river canyons for the winter, as his people had done for generations. Winter winds did not bite so harshly in those sheltered areas and the cold was less intense in the canyon country marked by lava rock formations and topped with cured bunchgrass needed to sustain the tribe's horses and cattle. In winter camp, people told stories, and women made new clothes or mended old garments, sewed intricate beaded patterns on a favorite dress, or added designs to a new shirt for their husbands. The men built or repaired bows using mountain sheep horns, cleaned guns they had acquired, gambled by playing the old stick game of their ancestors, and talked of the future and how they could preserve their independence.

During the coldest days of the winter, Nez Percés held Guardian Spirit Dances, where young boys and girls who had undertaken spirit quests expressed themselves through their new spirit songs. It was a time to honor tribal traditions and strengthen their souls for a new year. All sat around the fires and listened to the storytelling of elders. Joseph had watched homesteaders building cabins on Indian lands that fall. Perhaps, as he settled into his own winter camp in the canyon, he believed the white settlers would leave the high, windswept plateau country for the season; possibly he thought they would not return. Certainly his father's warning continued ringing though his mind just as the small bell that had been placed upon the grave tinkled in the wind during that first winter after the old headman died.

Joseph's band followed the growth of plants in the spring of 1872, traveling in search of early-maturing wild potato and kouse roots to replenish food supplies drawn down during the long winter months. They rode horses and boats constructed of bent poles covered with hides across the roiling Snake and Salmon rivers so they could camp on the prairie where women gathered camas. They located their villages beside the rivers, taking advantage of the early salmon runs and holding ceremonies to give thanks for these first foods of the season and for the bounty of their land. With food supplies restored, they migrated back to the Wallowa high country, herding horses and cattle up the grassy, rock-strewn canyon walls to mountain pastures where the air remained cool even as heat intensified in the gorges. Back in their own territory, they pitched lodges in places known to them and to their fore-bears, and they saw with astonishment and rising anger not only the two settlers Keith and McCormack in homestead cabins but other white people as well.

The Nez Percés argued about the situation among them-selves, suggesting and rejecting options before peaceably ap-proaching the settlers. Chief Joseph quietly told the whites they were on Indian land and that they would have to leave.

The whites stayed.

Joseph demanded that they join him in a formal council in mid-August 1872. There, backed by fifty non-treaty Nez Per-cés, including Eagle-From-the-Light, who served as his men-tor now that his father was gone, Joseph employed Chinook Jargon to again tell the settlers that they must leave his lands. Settler Joseph Johnson, who understood the trade language and became translator as well as spokesman for the intruders, said the 1863 treaty had transferred the land from Indian control to the government and argued that settlers had the right to live and farm in the Wallowa Valley. Joseph insisted that was not the case since his father had never sold the land. Finally, Johnson asked the question all the settlers feared: Would Joseph take up arms to force them to leave?

The young chief did not want blood spilled in his beloved

Wallowa Valley, so he answered Johnson honestly: he would not wage war, but he insisted they must leave.

Agent Monteith, learning of the settler–Indian meeting in the Wallowa, came to the area himself, arriving on horseback a week later. Joseph told the agent that the whites must not expand their presence in the valley because they damaged Mother Earth by cutting the grasses that represented her hair and by digging the soil that symbolized her body.

Monteith abhorred the Nez Percé Dreamer beliefs, considering them heathen practices. Like the missionaries before him, he preached Christianity and wanted the Indians to stop roaming the countryside hunting and gathering and to settle down in one spot and become farmers. While Monteith personally wondered if the 1863 treaty had honestly extinguished Indian title to the lands of the Wallowa Valley, as a representative of the government he told Joseph and the settlers "as far as I know from laws and treaties, the country was sold to the government, . . . it had been surveyed and brought into the market, and the government would protect the settlers."

Joseph renounced Monteith's statement: "If we ever owned the land, we own it still, for we never sold it."

Monteith, Joseph, and the settlers did not resolve the issues during that joint meeting, but they reached a tenuous understanding that neither whites nor Indians would be removed from the area—at least for the present. His nerves somewhat settled and feeling fairly confident that Joseph would not wage outright war against the settlers, Monteith rode back to Lapwai.

But of course the conflict was only tamped down; the underlying problem remained: Somebody had to leave the Wallowa country.

Late in 1872, the agent and the chief met again at the former's insistence. "I did not want to come to this council," Joseph told Monteith, "but I came hoping that we could save blood. The white man has no right to take our country. We have never accepted presents from the government. Neither Lawyer nor any other chief had authority to sell this land. It has always belonged to my people. It came to them from our fathers. . . . We will defend this land as long as a drop of Indian blood warms the hearts of our men."

It sounded like a declaration of war, but Joseph did not want to spill Indian or white blood and for the next six years made every effort to keep from doing so.

In what must have seemed like a breakthrough for Joseph and his people, Monteith, in late 1872, appeared to take their side. "It is a great pity that the valley was ever opened for settlement," the agent wrote the Commissioner of Indian Affairs in Washington. "If there is any way by which the Wallowa Valley could be kept for the Indians, I would recommend that it be done." In Salem, T. B. Odeneal, Oregon's Superintendent of Indian Affairs, read the report, and with his Washington, D.C., superiors he also began backing the tribesmen. With Monteith and Odeneal now appearing to support the long-held Indian position that they owned the Wallowa Valley, Joseph might have begun to hope the issue would be resolved in his people's favor. But other events that ought to have had nothing to do with the Nez Percé issues got in the way. Specifically, some Modoc Indians years before had left their

reservation in southern Oregon and returned to their homelands in California. When cavalry troops were dispatched to
California in 1872 to round up the Modocs and return them
to the reservation, the Indians resisted the attempt and took
refuge in a lava bed. There was a short, intense period of
fighting that left a peace commissioner dead and ended with
capture of the hostile Modocs. In retribution, authorities
hanged many of them in October 1873 and removed the remainder of the tribe to Indian Territory. The incident would
have lasting repercussions for the Nez Percés by solidifying
resentment toward all free-ranging Indians and stepping up
pressure to force them onto reservations.

As a result, instead of working out an agreement to recognize the Wallowa Valley as Indian land Odeneal and Monteith now had orders from their superiors to move Chief
Joseph and his band onto the reservation at Lapwai as provided by the 1863 treaty. These orders fell apart when the
agent and superintendent met face-to-face with Joseph on
March 27, 1873, and the powerfully persuasive chief convinced them that the 1863 treaty truly wasn't binding upon
his people. The government men thereupon decided they
would scuttle efforts to move Joseph and instead find ways to
allow him and his band to stay.

"The question for the Government to decide is as to
whether the title of these Indians was extinguished by the so-
called supplementary treaty of 1863, in which they took no
part," Monteith and Odeneal wrote in their 1873 report to
the Commissioner of Indian Affairs. They suggested that
perhaps, as Chief Joseph had so adamantly stated, the treaty
did not apply to the Wallowa Band, since Old Joseph had left
the council before its approval. "If so, then Wallowa Valley is

still part of the Nez Percé reservation; this being the case, then the Government is equitably bound to pay the white settlers for their improvements and for the trouble, inconvenience and expenses of removing," they wrote.

Success for Joseph seemed certain when, on April 30, 1873, a letter from Acting Commissioner of Indian Affairs H. R. Clum to Odeneal noted that the paperwork would soon be ready for President Grant's signature setting aside the Wallowa Valley for the exclusive use of the Nez Percés and prohibiting whites from entering or settling there.

When Joseph heard of that message, his people must have had a victory dance in their camp. It appeared they had, through his skilled diplomacy, preserved their homeland.

Governmental bureaucracy moved with unaccustomed speed. On May 10, General Land Office Commissioner W. W. Curtis issued orders to prevent further white settlement in the valley. In early June the executive order was forwarded to President Grant for his signature, but in identifying the boundaries for Indians and white settlers the locations had been reversed, giving the land most suited to Indian habitation to the whites and vice versa. The President signed the order, creating more of a muddle than before, as settler and Indian livestock mixed, causing increasing conflict between the two sides. The drumbeats of the Nez Percé victory dance quickly faded.

While Joseph and his people were perplexed by the new boundaries, the newspapers of the region vented the fury of white settlers. "Those who have not heard the news . . . giving the Wallowa Valley to the Indians, will almost be struck dumb with the intelligence that such is the case," thundered the *Mountain Sentinel,* published in Grande Ronde, Oregon. The blame for such action, the *Sentinel* charged, lay with Odeneal. He "stinks in the nostrils of every decent man east of the Cascades for the dirty part he has acted in robbing the settlers of Wallowa of their homes, their everything," the writer said. "Were he today to put in an appearance among those whom he has so foully wronged, [Odeneal] would pay the penalty with his worthless life."

Government agents meantime began collecting information necessary to remove the settlers, learning it would cost $67,860 to pay for "improvements." Despite the *Sentinel*'s angry editorials, many settlers wanted to sell out and leave the Wallowa, finding the valley a difficult place to make a living.

The man who ended any hope for a peaceful resolution of the conflict was Oregon governor Lafayette F. Grover, who had been besieged with letters and visits from people supporting white settlement in the valley. He dispatched a letter containing a clear distortion of the issues to Secretary of the Interior Columbus Delano. Not only did Grover say that Old Joseph and his band had taken government annuities under terms of the 1855 treaty negotiated at Walla Walla—when they did not—but he also claimed that Joseph's followers did not want the Wallowa Valley for a reservation and home. He urged Delano, who had no understanding at all of the Nez Percé case, to rescind the executive order establishing the Indian claim to the region.

Facing pressure not only from Oregon's governor and the state's congressional delegation, Delano waffled. Instead of implementing the executive order, he instructed Monteith and Odeneal to restudy the situation. In March 1873, a three-man team appointed by the Commissioner of Indian Affairs got involved, and while there appeared to be initial support for Joseph's position, by the fall of 1873 the wind had shifted again. This time Monteith wrote: "The Department cannot too soon take the necessary steps toward those living outside the reservation . . . the Treaty of 1863 . . . provides for the [relocation] of the Indians and it should be done at as early a day as possible."

Unsettled by the constantly changing position of the local agent, Joseph, now beginning to realize that decisions came from Washington, asked if he might visit the President of the United States to present his case. When Monteith denied this request, Joseph stormed away from Lapwai, gathering his people for another winter in the canyons. In the spring of 1874, he found that although President Grant's 1873 executive order establishing a territory for the Nez Percés in part of the Wallowa Valley remained in force, there would be no further effort to establish a reservation there for his band.

Political pressure had trumped Joseph's persuasive arguments. U.S. Commissioner of Indian Affairs Edwin P. Smith wrote Oregon senator James K. Kelly to inform him "the whole valley is now open for settlement."

This was another deception, and one that Joseph did not even learn about for a year. Even so, it was becoming difficult for the chief to maintain order. Young men within his band did not like the uncertainty of their tribal position. They wanted to fight, and it was all Joseph and Ollokot could do to maintain the peace.

A summer gathering in 1874 at Split Rocks, south of the Camas Prairie and a site often used as a council ground for Nez Percés, brought together many of the anti-treaty bands. Looking Glass, son of the elder man of the same name, who had assumed his father's role as headman, and respected Nez

Percé warriors Five Wounds, Grizzly Bear, and Rainbow agreed with Joseph and Ollokot that war would not help them retain their lands. They would continue to rely on diplomacy. Wallowa Band members returned home from the council to find their lands dotted with even more white-owned homesteads. The Indians found it impossible to keep free-ranging cattle and horses from intermingling with the settlers' animals. But a tenuous peace prevailed.

During this period there were few major disagreements between the Indian and white factions of the Wallowa region. Joseph got to know many of the intruders, visiting their homes, taking meals with them, conversing in Chinook Jargon, and playing with their children. The settlers who met him described him as patient, kind, and intelligent. War leader Ollokot, his brother's strongest ally, also visited with the settlers, who sometimes confused the two, at times calling both of them Joseph, though the chief was more sedate than his high-spirited younger brother.

"Joseph put his large black eyes on my face, and maintained a fixed look for some time. It did not appear to me as an audacious stare, but I thought he was trying to open the windows of his heart to me," Major General Oliver O. Howard wrote of his first encounter with Chief Joseph in the spring of 1875 on the Umatilla reservation northwest of the Wallowa Valley.

Said Joseph to the former Civil War general, now in command of the army's Department of the Columbia, headquartered at Fort Vancouver, "I heard that Washington had some message for me."

The general, who had headed the post-war Freedmen's Bureau and the man for whom Howard University, established in 1867, had been named, replied, "There is no word from Washington."

The two men shook hands and years later Howard would say, "I think Joseph and I became then quite good friends."

This from the man soon to become Chief Joseph's greatest nemesis.

What Joseph wanted in that first meeting with Howard was confirmation of a rumor floating across the Pacific Northwest that President Grant had rescinded his executive order establishing a reservation for the Nez Percé band in the Wallowa Valley. In truth, at that time Howard did not know, but on June 19, 1875, the new proclamation arrived. There would be no reservation for Joseph's band in their homeland: they were required to move to Idaho. When Monteith gave Joseph the news at agency headquarters at Lapwai, the chief's anger overflowed. He shouted about the inconsistent and unfair actions of the government, then leaped on his war horse and raced away with his strongest warriors, all using braided leather quirts to speed their own mounts. From Wallowa Joseph sent runners to the other anti-treaty bands, calling them to a council at Indian Town beneath the bluff where his father was buried.

Joseph was not alone in his anger upon hearing the news. The old Dreamer Toolhoolhoolzote demanded an immediate hostile response; White Bird and Eagle-from-the-Light agreed it might now be time to fight. But Joseph, his initial fury spent and with emotions now under control, once again argued for peace and diplomacy and, with support from Ollokot and Looking Glass, began calming the fury of other non-treaty bands. Support from spiritual leaders in the various bands for Joseph's non-violent position further eased the tension.

In maintaining the peace despite tremendous setbacks and pressure from prominent leaders in his tribe to fight, Joseph again gained support and admiration from federal authorities. Captain Stephen G. Whipple, commanding two companies of cavalry sent to the area during the height of tensions that year, wrote General Howard to say that the Wallowa tribesmen "are by no means a vagabond set. They are proud-spirited, self-supporting and intelligent." He told his superior the area was suitable only for raising livestock and even that was difficult because of its long winters. Relying on Whipple's recommendations, Howard supported Chief Joseph's claim to the Wallowa. He wrote: "I think it is a great mistake to take from Joseph and his band of Nez Percés Indians that valley. The white people really do not want it . . . possibly Congress can be induced to let these really peaceable Indians have this poor valley for their own."

While the Wallow Valley may have been considered "poor" to Howard, for Joseph it was home and he would continue to fight for it. "That [valley] had always belonged to my father's own people, and the other bands had never disputed our right to it," he said. "No other Indians ever claimed Wallowa. Our fathers were born here. Here they lived, here they died, here are their graves. We will never leave them."

Two other independent investigations of Joseph's claim to the valley had similar conclusions: the Nez Percés had not relinquished claim to the land.

Howard's assistant adjutant general, Henry Clay Wood, who had "read medicine" before studying the law and passing his bar exam in his native Maine twenty years earlier, conducted an inquiry into the issue at Howard's request. In January 1876, Wood wrote: "In my opinion the non-treaty Nez Percés cannot in law be regarded as bound by the treaty of 1863; and in so far as it attempts to deprive them of a right to occupancy of any land its provisions are null and void. The extinguishment of their title of occupancy contemplated by this treaty is imperfect and incomplete. . . . It remains for the commissioner of Indian Affairs to solve the problem of a politic and just disposition of the non-treaty Nez Percés." Later Wood added: "Until Joseph commits some overt act of hostility, force should not be used to put him on any reservation."

Reverend A. L. Lindsley, a prominent Presbyterian from Portland who had close communications with Monteith at Lapwai, agreed. "Title has never been rightfully extinguished," the minister said in a letter to Howard. "In fact, the fair construction of treaty stipulations confirms the Indian title."

The seesaw continued. Each time Joseph thought life might settle into a comfortable pattern, something upset the balance, and each time it became harder for the tribal leader to tip it back to his side. On June 22, 1876, just three days before the battle at the Little Bighorn in Montana's buffalo country, white settlers A. B. Findley and Wells McNall killed Wind Blowing, a Wallowa tribesman, in a dispute over horses near Whiskey Creek not far from Indian Town. After the killing, the settlers returned to their homes while the Indians took Wind Blowing's body back to their camp for burial. Joseph mourned the death of the man he considered a brother, then rode to Lapwai to demand that the culprits face justice. Monteith told Joseph not to take action on his own and said he would have civil authorities deal with the incident. The agent characterized the death as "willful, deliberate murder" when he asked Captain David L. Perry, the thirty-six-year-old Connecticut native in command of two companies of the First U.S. Cavalry at Lapwai, to go to Wallowa to preserve the peace.

After he learned of the killing, O. O. Howard ordered his assistant adjutant general, Henry Clay Wood, to investigate. Wood reached Lapwai a month after Wind Blowing's death, and there Joseph told him his friend's life "was worth more than the Wallowa Valley." But since the earth there had "drunk up" Wind Blowing's blood, Joseph said, the valley was more sacred to him than ever before and now he claimed it "as recompense for the life taken." Again Joseph insisted the white settlers must leave.

Wood told Joseph that General Howard had recommended a five-member council be appointed in Washington to come to Lapwai and settle the landownership question once and for all. Finally, Wood told Joseph not to take action on the murder because civil authorities would handle it. Somewhat mollified, the chief returned to Wallowa, but two months later, when there had been no action against McNall and Findley by civil authorities, Joseph and Ollokot forced the issue. Dressed for battle, they swooped over the hills on their war horses, surrounded settler cabins, and told the occupants they had to leave their homes within days and that if Findley and McNall did not give themselves up, blood would flow in the valley. As a result of this ultimatum, Wind Blowing's killers turned themselves in to authorities, defusing the situation. No charge was ever filed against McNall; Findley was acquitted after claiming self-defense. Within weeks both settlers returned to their homesteads. Most of the other settlers remained as well.

"I labored hard to avoid trouble and bloodshed," Joseph would later say. "We gave up some of our country to the white men, thinking that then we could have peace. We were mistaken. The white men could not let us alone. We could have avenged our wrongs many times, but we did not. When the white men were few and we were strong, we could have killed them off, but the Nez Percés wish to live in peace."

Meanwhile, authorities in Washington approved the new commission Howard had sought and the five officials reached Lapwai in November. Joseph met with them and passionately asked that his people be allowed to stay in the Wallowa country, for the earth "was sacred to his affections, too sacred to be valued by or sold for silver and gold." His dignified, though animated, eloquence moved the commissioners but also irritated them because they could not shake his convictions.

Howard later wrote that the Nez Percés "were offered everything they wanted, if they would simply submit to the authority and government of the United States Agents."

But they refused.

"All I have to say is that I love my country," Joseph told the commissioners.

Howard asked, "Suppose several thousand men should come from Oregon with arms, what would you do?"

"We will not sell the land. We will not give up the land," Joseph said.

It Was Now War in Earnest

our Indians rode frost-coated horses across the Snake River in early January 1877, bringing a message from Agent Monteith to Joseph's canyon camp where he was snug against winter winds and snow. Present at the meeting were Joseph's father-in-law, Whisk-tasket; his sister's husband, Reuben, headman at Lapwai since the death of Lawyer a year earlier; nephew James Reuben, who spoke English and Nez Percé and served as an interpreter at the agency; and another treaty Indian. The Indian messengers had information they knew would anger the Wallowa headman. Finding seats in the smoky warmth of Joseph's longhouse lodge, they told him that the November commission had submitted its final report: He and his people, fifty men of fighting age and more than three times that many old men, women, and children, had until April 1 to relocate onto the reservation.

Such a move meant packing up a winter camp and gathering stock during the coldest, most disagreeable weather of the year. Joseph had no intention of complying. His response mirrored previous statements he'd made: "I have been talking to the whites many years about the land in question, and it is strange they cannot understand me," he told Reuben. "The country they claim belonged to my father, and when he died it was given to me and my people, and I will not leave it until I am compelled to."

O. O. Howard, comfortable in his quarters at Fort Vancouver near the Pacific Coast, opened a January 13, 1877, letter from General Irwin McDowell, commander of the Division of the Pacific at San Francisco, and settled into his chair as he read the orders. "As this question of the removal of Joseph's band is a very delicate and important one," McDowell wrote, "the division commander directs it to be done under your personal direction if practicable."

Howard had not been in the field since 1872, when he and two aides had cornered the Apache chief Cochise in Arizona, leading to his surrender. Now Howard would give up the comfort of a warm bed, full meals, an upholstered chair, and a solid writing desk, in order to orchestrate the removal of a band of Indians who had for years fought to remain in their country. This message to remove the Nez Percés from Wallowa came after Agent Monteith heard Joseph's negative reaction to the order to peacefully relocate to the reservation, and it was no surprise to Howard. He had a hand in formulating the commission response just issued. Among the recommendations: leading Nez Percé Dreamers would be "suppressed" or, better yet, exiled to Indian Territory; military occupation would occur at Wallowa until Joseph's band relocated to the reservation at Lapwai; force could be used against the Indians who failed to move quickly and peacefully or if any Indians caused disturbances; and finally, once on the reservation, the non-treaty Indians would be treated similarly to those who supported the 1863 agreement.

Howard now had orders to deal with the Nez Percé removal but knew he must proceed cautiously, for his superiors instructed him to pressure Joseph into moving, rather than resort to force.

On November 25, 1876, just days after the council at Lapwai had concluded and the five commissioners began preparing their final report on the Nez Percé landownership claims, frontier army troops far to the east of the Continental Divide in Wyoming struck the mountain camp of Cheyenne Indians led by Dull Knife. They pounded the village in a brutal attack, forcing the Cheyennes out of their winter lodges and into bitter high country weather as they fled north toward the village of Lakota chief Crazy Horse. The army had never had much patience with free-ranging Indians; these troops had even less in the aftermath of the Little Bighorn battle in June 1876, where Crazy Horse and Oglala medicine man Sitting Bull, with their Cheyenne allies, annihilated 215 troopers of Lieutenant Colonel George A. Custer's Seventh Cavalry.

Following the late November 1876 attack on Dull Knife's band, frontier troops began reorganizing on the northern plains of Wyoming and Montana. They would begin subduing other free-ranging Indians; none could be allowed to remain off reservations. Those troops would first subdue Crazy Horse's band, which now included some Dull Knife refugees, and force them all onto a reservation in Nebraska or remove them to Indian Territory. They would then accelerate demands for the surrender of Sitting Bull. The Hunkpapa leader and his followers had fled Little Bighorn the previous June and crossed into Canada, where they regrouped in a camp in the hills of southern Saskatchewan. Their action had given other Indians the idea that freedom might lie north of the Medicine Line, as the native people referred to the border between the United States and Canada.

On March 17, at Joseph's behest, his brother and the band's war leader, Ollokot, rode to Lapwai, where he told Agent Monteith the Indians had no desire to fight the army or anyone else. "I have eyes and a heart, and can see and understand for myself that if we fight we would have to leave all and go into the mountains," he said. "I love my wife and children and could not leave them."

Ollokot returned to Wallowa; then, as the April 1 removal deadline approached, Joseph sent him to meet General Howard on the Umatilla reservation. Ollokot told the general the Nez Percés were willing to share a reservation with the Umatillas, but that offer was quickly quashed. Howard bluntly said the Indians had to move to the reservation at Lapwai but agreed to one more meeting with the tribesmen.

Ollokot rode back to Joseph's camp, angry at the general's denial of their proposal to join the Umatillas, and told his brother they had few options. "If you say, 'Yes,'" he told Joseph, "I will bring in the stock and we will go [to Lapwai]."

Removal of the non-treaty Nez Percés for years had centered on Joseph's band. The Wallowa people had more wealth—cattle and horses—than the other bands, and that power, combined with Joseph's oratorical ability, made him the lead tribal spokesman and diplomat. Frontier newspapers in Oregon and Idaho outlined issues related to the Nez Percé landownership and ascribed to Joseph an authority over all Nez Percés that he simply did not have. Other tribesmen had a stake in the issue. Each band involved had its own headman and leadership and so retained autonomy. The tribe had occasionally designated one prominent man to speak for all of the bands, but it never recognized that individual as being supreme over all others, as did the frontier military and popular press of the period.

The 1863 treaty provisions that affected Joseph's territory also required removal of Nez Percés led by White Bird, Toolhoolhoolzote, and Looking Glass. Knowing those men would be at the Lapwai council Howard had agreed upon, Joseph prepared to make one final effort to retain the lands that held the bones of his father. He rode at the head of a single column of his men to Lapwai. They wore their finest cloth or buckskin leggings with contrasting cuffs and beadwork, breechclouts made of a woven multi-colored cloth shawl, and war shirts their wives had decorated with intricate beading. The men had multiple-loop strands of shell and bead necklaces around their necks and wore their long hair braided and pulled forward over their chests with pompadour standing upright. Their horses were bedecked with colorful saddle blankets, each unique to the man who owned it, making the men and animals distinctive and recognizable. Feather headstalls were placed over the forelocks of many horses, and woven horsehair tassels swung under their necks.

At Lapwai the riders circled the post three times, then dismounted. They handed their horses off to younger men who would care for them, and piled their guns and other weapons at the post gate in a symbolic statement: councils were for talk and discussion, not physical action.

This "splendid looking Indian," as Emily FitzGerald, wife of the Fort Lapwai doctor, had described Joseph just months earlier, entered a large hospital tent erected to serve as the council meeting area. Ollokot walked with him. They were the first Nez Percé leaders to reach the council site and reluctantly met Howard, finally convincing the general they would only talk freely when the other headmen arrived.

On May 3, the council reconvened. Six-foot-tall White Bird, though in his seventies, showed vigor in his brisk walk to the council tent. He carried an eagle wing symbolic of his Dreamer medicine leader status over some fifty families. Looking Glass, in his mid-forties, lean and tall, was spokesman for some forty families, most of whom already lived on reservation lands. The final headman at the council was old Toolhoolhoolzote, the Dreamer who had been involved in treaty councils at Walla Walla in 1855 and at Lapwai in 1863. FitzGerald called him a "ferocious looking old medicine man (an old, old man)," while Howard said he was "broad-shouldered, deep-chested, thick-necked."

"The men's faces were painted, the red paint extending back into the partings of their hair," Howard said. The Indians had braided their hair and were "ornamented in dress, in hats, in blankets with variegated colors, in leggings of buckskin and beaded and plain moccasins."

The old Dreamer, who had thirty families in his band, became lead spokesman for all the headmen. "I have heard about a bargain," Toolhoolhoolzote told Howard in a deeply gut-tural voice, "a trade between some of these Indians and the white men concerning the land."

Howard responded that the Nez Percés had traded lands and now the minority bands—the non-treaties represented by those present—must abide by the agreement. Tension in the hospital tent became palpable as the general, known to the Indians as Cut Off Arm, and the Dreamer traded barbs.

"The Great Spirit Chief made the world as it is and as he wanted it, and he made a part of it for us to live upon," Tool-hoolhoolzote said to murmurs of agreement from the others. "I do not see where you get authority to say that we shall not live where he placed us."

Howard realized he could not bring the issue to a conclu-sion in the tense atmosphere the Dreamer had created, and so delayed talks for two days. During that period he sent an or-der to Fort Walla Walla for troops to move closer to the Wal-lowa Valley. He would be prepared should trouble erupt.

Joseph learned of the troop movement before the talks re-sumed, and both he and Ollokot realized the situation was becoming dire. Most of Joseph's able-bodied warriors had accompanied him to Lapwai, and their families remained un-protected in the Wallowa. As talks resumed, Toolhoolhool-zote picked up his arguments where he had left off days before, sharply telling Howard the earth should not be plowed or taken from the various bands: "You white people get together, measure the earth, and then divide it," the man Howard later called a "cross-grained growler" insisted.

The religious general had heard enough. He would listen to no more from the Indians about their relationship with the earth. He insisted they must move to the reservation. Tool-hoolhoolzote made a final demand: "What person pretends to divide the land, and put me on it?"

Angry now, Howard barked out his answer: "I am the man. I stand here for the President, and there is no spirit god or band that will hinder me. My orders are plain, and will be executed."

The Dreamer said he would not move to the reservation, and others in the council tent muttered in agreement. Howard could stand no more. "This bad advice is what you give the Indians," he thundered. "On account of it, you will have to be taken to the Indian territory . . . [and] I will send you there if it takes years and years." Allowing no further response, Howard and First Cavalry captain David Perry took Tool-hoolhoolzote by the arm, ushered him from the council, and locked him in the guardhouse. The action shocked and angered the Nez Percés. Joseph's warriors tensed for an immediate attack, prompting him to rise from his seat.

"I am going to talk now. I don't care whether you arrest me or not," he told the remaining white negotiators. Then he faced his own people, telling them the Dreamer's arrest was wrong, but directed, "We will not resent the insult. We were invited to this council to express our hearts, and we have done so."

Years later Joseph again spoke of the tense moments following the Dreamer's arrest and his warriors' reaction. "I counseled them to submit," he said. "I knew if we resisted that all the white men present, including General Howard, would be killed in a moment, and we would be blamed."

Before the council adjourned, Howard gave the final ultimatum: Joseph and the others had ten days to report to the reservation. This impossible deadline stunned Joseph. He had just forded the Snake and Salmon in coming to Lapwai and knew the rivers were approaching full crest, roiling from bank to bank with snowmelt. "I notice that when you want to move it takes a long time to do it, especially when there are rivers to cross," he told Howard, reminding the general that his people resided west of the two rivers. "We want time," he said. "Ten days is no time for us. We have plenty of children, women, horses, and cattle, and the rivers are high."

"I want no humbugging," Howard commanded, "Do as I tell you to do—move immediately to the reserve."

During the next few days Howard rode across the reservation lands with Joseph so the Wallowa headman could select a place for his people to live when they relocated. Joseph found only one site he liked, and a few Indians and some white people already had homes there. When Howard told him he would remove the settlers, Joseph said, "It would be wrong to disturb these people. I have no right to take their homes. I have never taken what did not belong to me. I will not now."

By May 14 White Bird and Looking Glass convinced Howard to release Toolhoolhoolzote from the guardhouse, saying they would be responsible for his behavior. Howard also relaxed his relocation order. Instead of ten days he gave Joseph and the other Nez Percé chiefs thirty days to return to their lands, gather widely scattered horses and cattle, pack up their villages, and return to the reservation. Only Looking Glass was exempt from the rapid-fire removal, since his band already camped on the reservation. Howard granted Husis Kute, or Naked Head, a Palouse ally who would relocate to the reservation with them, thirty-five days to make his move from his more remote lands in Washington.

In Wallowa a mood of despondency hung over Joseph's camp as the women organized belongings for the departure. They were used to packing up the camp; several times each year they followed wild plant–harvesting routines and migrated between summer and winter villages. But this move was urgent and complex, since all the people, from tiny babies to the most elderly men and women, some of whom could barely walk, were to move at once, taking as many belongings as they could tie onto their packhorses. Meantime, men and boys began the impossible task of rounding up all the livestock that had been grazing virtually unattended throughout the winter.

By early June, Joseph's people began their exodus to the reservation. In spurts, they rode toward the benchland at a well-known Nez Percé ford on the Snake River, setting up a new camp at Dug Bar, upstream from the mouth of the Imnaha and below the deep, narrow canyon. Joseph and his warriors had crossed at Dug Bar a couple of weeks earlier, but this fording would be more hazardous. The river was near peak flood stage, and little children and old people could not ride swimming horses across the raging waters as the men did. Some men and boys continued to locate livestock and others built small boats of green poles bent and covered with hides.

Finally, it was time to assault the current. The strongest men stripped to their breechclouts and rode the most powerful horses into the wild water that crashed and cascaded against the boulder-strewn riverbed and canyon walls as they angled their mounts next to those bearing able-bodied women and older children. There was a solid rock wall directly across the river from their entry point, but from experience they knew the current would force them downstream to a sloping grass-covered bank where they could find an exit. They also knew that the river here swirled in a whirlpool manner, the current switching direction near the sides of the canyon. Initially the horses were forced upstream when they entered the river, before the swift water caught them and pulled them downriver and across its span until a new eddy helped them to safely reach the eastern riverbank. This river current worked the same way when horseback riders tied ropes to the boats and pulled them across the river. Naked swimmers held on to the boats to further guide them.

The first people to ford the Snake set up a new camp and prepared food for the men who were making multiple trips across the river to assist the others. Children and the elderly crossed in boats piled high with clothing, food, camp equipment, and the lodges and home furnishings of the tribesmen. The men who rode back and forth through the raging current changed horses often, since the fierce roil of water quickly drained the animals of energy. As the last Nez Percé campfires on the Wallowa homeland died down, those on the reservation side of the Snake began sending tendrils of smoke into the canyon.

Once the people were safely across the river, the arduous task of moving livestock took all the attention and skill of the Nez Percé horsemen. As they forced the cattle and horses into the fast current, the healthy adult animals, aided by the force of the eddies, swam through the swift waters, but the current tipped and pulled under calves and foals, plus adult animals that were weak or pregnant. Hundreds did not make it out of the river but were swept downstream, where they were pounded against rocks and washed up onto sandbars or benchlands broken, bleeding, and dead. At Wallowa, white settlers claimed the hundreds of head of livestock the Nez Percés had been unable to gather in those frantic days of removal.

After the Snake River crossing on May 31, 1877, Joseph's band regrouped and rode up the steep grass-covered hillside on the east side of the Snake at Dug Bar before descending into the Salmon River canyon, where they again challenged white water. By June 11 they had reached the lake campsite near Split Rocks, a place the tribes often met for council and to gather camas roots. There they joined the bands of White Bird and Toolhoolhoolzote, plus the Indians led by Naked Head, their Palouse ally. He had sixteen men. The camp soon had nearly 700 people who had come together for a final few days of freedom.

Joseph, Ollokot, and several others left the camp soon after they arrived, returning to the Salmon River and crossing it to slaughter the cattle they had left on the west side. Joseph's twelve-year-old daughter and Ollokot's wife, Wetatonmi, accompanied them to help butcher the meat. Joseph's second wife, Springtime, remained in her lodge, a structure isolated from the rest of the camp, because she expected to give birth at any time.

Two days before the Nez Percés were due on the reservation, their big camp at the lake bustled with activity. Women began preparing freshly harvested kouse roots to replace food supplies dwindled during the long winter months. Older children watched toddlers to keep them from interfering with the work of their mothers. Old men and women sat on blankets or hides, their bodies supported by woven backrests as they visited with people from differing bands whom they had not seen in many months.

The warriors added pageantry to the atmosphere as they held a final parade before moving to the reservation. Older, more battle-seasoned warriors, wearing their finest garb and riding horses outfitted with feathered forelock headstalls and multi-colored saddle blankets or pads made from the hides of wolves and cougars, took the lead as drums pounded and both men and women sang and chanted. The men rode around the camp and waved their shields made of the tough hide from a buffalo's neck or several layers of elk rawhide stretched over a frame and covered with softly tanned leather that was painted and decorated with war honors. They brandished weapons while the manes and tails of their horses whipped in motion to their rocking gait.

Shore Crossing, one of the young riders at the end of the warrior parade, unintentionally caused his horse to step into the work area of a Nez Percé woman preparing kouse roots. The woman's husband confronted Shore Crossing and told the young man that he should avenge the death of Shore Crossing's father, Eagle Robe, who had been killed by a white settler named Larry Ott three years earlier. In other circumstances such a challenge might have easily faded, but not on the day before these free-spirited people would give up their freedom.

That evening Shore Crossing and his warrior partner Red Moccasin Tops took their weapons, painted their foreheads red, added war markings to their horses, and quietly rode from camp, determined to kill Larry Ott. They took Shore

Crossing's nephew, Swan Necklace, with them to hold the horses without telling him of their mission. Shore Crossing and his partner could not find their intended victim but were not deterred from their revenge ride. By the time they returned to camp the two young warriors had murdered four Salmon River settlers and stolen their horses.

General O. O. Howard and Agent John Monteith knew of the Indian gathering at the lake and presumed they would reach the reservation, just a few miles to the north, by June 14, the end of Howard's thirty-day deadline. Joseph and Ollokot, killing cattle at the Salmon River, also expected to make a peaceful move onto the reservation. The big camp on the morning of that fateful day, however, was in near chaos as White Bird and Toolhoolhoolzote learned that Shore Crossing and Red Moccasin Tops had touched the spark to the tinder that led to war. Upon hearing of the killings, other men donned war attire, grabbed their weapons, and rode from camp on painted and decorated horses. During the next two days they roamed the Salmon River country and rode north onto the Camas Prairie, where they killed a dozen or more settlers, caused others to gather for mutual protection, and spurred white messengers to ride north to request army intervention.

After those first fierce raids—all waged against men who had earlier had conflicts with the Nez Percés—the warriors returned to the Tolo Lake campsite, which was named for Tolo, a Nez Perce woman who had warned some settlers before the raids.

Joseph's party, leading a dozen pack horses laden with freshly killed beef toward the lake, met a warrior en route who told them, "War has broke out. Three white men killed yester-day!" Actually, four settlers had died in the original raid, and even more since then.

The party raced to the camp, where Joseph pleaded with his tribesmen, "Let us stay here till the army comes! We will then make some kind of peace with them." But the tribesmen rebuffed him, packed their possessions, and rode southeast to White Bird Canyon.

"I was deeply grieved," Joseph said, "All the lodges were moved except my brother's and my own. I saw clearly that the war was upon us when I learned that my young men had been secretly buying ammunition."

Joseph and Ollokot had kept their young warriors from re-acting violently to white incursions and attacks for years but knew now there would be no restraint. The Nez Percés "had been insulted a thousand times. Their fathers and brothers had been killed; their mothers and wives had been disgraced," Joseph later said. Other issues contributed to the attacks on the Salmon River settlers during June 13, 14, and 15, not the least of which was learning that white settlers were claiming any horses and cattle the Indians could not gather and move to the reservation.

"I would have given my own life if I could have undone the killing of white men by my people," Joseph said. "I blame my young men and I blame the white men. I blame General Howard for not giving my people time to get their stock away from Wallowa."

Standing on the brink of full-scale war and no longer in the Wallowa Valley, Joseph was enveloped in despair. When he and Ollokot did not immediately move to White Bird Canyon, other warriors stayed nearby watching to see that

Joseph did not go onto the reservation as they feared, now that hostilities had begun. Joseph told them his "blood was on fire" because of the attacks and he would remain aligned with the non-treaty bands even as he denied that the Wallowa belonged to anyone outside his band: "It is still our land. It may never again be our home, but my father sleeps there, and I love it as I love my mother. I left there hoping to avoid bloodshed."

Unable to camp near Looking Glass on the Clearwater because that leader did not want to be drawn into the conflict, Joseph and Ollokot moved south with the other non-treaty bands to White Bird Canyon along the Salmon River in Idaho. There the Nez Percé headmen talked of ways they might avert further violence but knew it was now almost certain they would face the guns of General Howard's soldiers.

During their raiding and killing spree, some Nez Percés found barrels and crocks of whiskey and brought them on the night of June 16 to their hastily erected camp along White Bird Creek, where they drummed and danced and drank far into the night.

Word of the killings at Salmon River and Camas Prairie reached the army at Fort Lapwai, seventy miles to the north, on June 15. Immediately troops from Companies F and H, United States First Cavalry, under command of Captain David L. Perry, a veteran of the Modoc War in California five years earlier, climbed into their saddles for a forced march south. They carried in their saddlebags the standard three days' issue of rations: hardtack, jerked or dried meat, and coffee. They had tobacco for their pipes, a tin cup, spoon and knife, canteen, and a tin pot or used peach can with a wire handle for coffee making. On the backs of their saddles they tied their canvas shelter tents and wool blankets. Pack horses carried enough additional food to support the companies in the field another five days.

The troopers were issued two weapons: a Model 1875 Springfield .45 caliber single-shot carbine and a Model 1873 Colt .45 revolver and holster. Each man was also issued a leather carbine sling and twenty cartridges for each weapon held in the new-style leather cartridge belts with canvas tabs for the shells. They wore blue army uniforms, wool greatcoats, black campaign hats, leather boots, and leather gauntlets to protect their wrists and arms.

On the north side of the Camas Prairie the cavalrymen took one of their short breaks at Norton's Ranch on Cotton-wood Creek, where they unsaddled their horses to let them graze for an hour, kindled small fires to make coffee, and chewed on hardtack or a piece of dried meat. There was no time for sleep, as frantic settlers rode into their camp begging them to move south quickly. The troops caught and saddled horses, then swung into the seats for another twenty-mile ride in the dark with volunteer citizen guides.

The troops, tired from their two-day march, halted below the crest of a hill and waited through the coldest hours of the night, then, at dawn on June 17, moved to the hilltop but could not see the thirty lodges of the Nez Percé camp, lying along White Bird Creek and hidden behind a series of steep hills.

The Nez Percés were aware of the cavalrymen—warned by their Indian pickets—and the headmen sent forth six warriors carrying a white flag in a final effort to talk rather than fight. These six men were instructed to negotiate with the troop commanders and to surrender those responsible for the recent settler killings in order to avoid confrontation. When the men carrying the white flags were mid-way up the grassy hillside they saw Arthur "Ad" Chapman, one of the earliest settlers on White Bird Creek, who as a volunteer with the army had led the cavalry to their location. Some of the Indians recognized Chapman, who was married to an Indian woman, spoke their language, and had often visited their camps. As Chapman came over the brink of the hill and saw the Indians he disregarded their flag of truce and fired the first shot of what became known as the Nez Percé War. The Indian negotiators found cover in brush on the hillside and then responded to the gunfire with their own repeating rifles, pistols, and muzzle-loading muskets. Sixty other Nez Percés soon joined the fight.

Captain Perry now ordered First Cavalry Company F forward to join a skirmish line of Twenty-first Infantry troopers led by Lieutenant Edward Russell Theller, a Vermont native. The one hundred soldiers along White Bird Canyon had the high ground, but the sixty warriors facing them were hidden in heavy brush. Within minutes, some Nez Percés organized by Ollokot rode up the steep hillside and surrounded Theller's men. Indians also quickly positioned themselves before Perry's cavalry line, raking the horse soldiers in a withering fire that caused them to break ranks, flee into a draw, and then retreat up another steep hillside. The Indians pressed their attack, many of them armed only with bows and arrows. As the soldiers, including Theller and most of his men, fell in the hail of well-placed gunfire, the Indian men and women took the carbines from their bodies and stripped off their ammunition belts.

The mounted Nez Percés were superb riders compared to many of the cavalrymen they faced. When the warriors' horses tired, they changed to new animals held at the ready by Nez Percé women. The soldiers, many of them inept riders to begin with, struggled to control horses that were jumpy and hard to manage in the midst of the gunfire, noise, and confusion caused by the loose horses of the Nez Percés. Added to the soldiers' problems was the fact that many of them had not tightened their cinches prior to descending the canyon. This caused their saddles to turn and spilled riders to the ground as the horses became agitated.

The chaos in the army command was magnified in the opening moments of the fighting when Nez Percé marksmen killed the army buglers, making it nearly impossible for commanders to provide instructions to their troops.

Before long most of the military were in retreat, some men moving in an orderly backtracking and in support of comrades, others racing pell-mell back up the hill as the Indians pursued. The soldiers, many of them on foot, tired quickly while Joseph and the Nez Percés, who had been climbing mountains steeper than these in their Wallowa and Salmon river homelands since they were toddlers, never faltered.

Intense fighting lasted only a few minutes, but Indians on horseback, led by Shore Crossing, Red Moccasin Tops, and Strong Eagle, each wearing a full-length red blanket coat that made him recognizable to his fellow warriors and a clear target to the soldiers, pressed the retreating troops. These men became known as the Three Red Coats and, supported by other fast-riding warriors, pursued the fleeing cavalry for nearly a dozen miles before returning to White Bird Canyon, where black powder smoke drifted across the battlefield.

Thirty-four soldiers had been killed. Indian men and women combed the battleground, picking up sixty-three carbines, some pistols, and ammunition and rounding up cavalry horses to add to their own herds.

Among the Nez Percés there were no dead and only three warriors had sustained wounds, all minor.

During the fighting that Sunday morning, several white people who had homes along White Bird Creek fled toward the soldiers. One man became the target of a warrior who shot an arrow at him but struck a young girl riding behind the man. The child cried out in pain and the Indian turned away. He later said, "Not used to killing, it hurt my feelings to hear that little child crying."

The rout at White Bird might have been even more spectacular if all the warriors in camp had participated. At least a third of them remained near their lodges suffering from the effects of their all-night drinking binge. After the battle at White Bird, none of the Indians had any delusions about settling peacefully at Lapwai.

Said Chief Joseph, "It was now war in earnest."

Beginning the Flight

The Nez Percés struck their camp and crossed the still-raging Salmon River, building boats as they had done at the Snake. This time, without the river eddies to help in the crossing, they tied four horses to the hide-covered vessels to tow them across the river while men swam alongside to stabilize the crafts. The boats carried huge loads of camp goods, with children and old people riding in precarious perches on top of the packs. Once over the river the Indians turned north following the long ridge above the Salmon and Snake river drainages. It was country Joseph, Toolhoolhoolzote, and White Bird knew intimately, although General Howard, arriving soon after the battle at White Bird Creek, believed he had the Nez Percés hemmed in. He wrote: "The longer . . . Joseph delays with his women, children and abundant stock of horses and cattle between the Salmon and the Snake, the more certain he is shut in."

The soldiers did not have Nez Percé experience in crossing raging rivers and so remained east of the Salmon and on June

26 finally buried the blackened, putrifying bodies of those who had died at White Bird Canyon nine days earlier. The following day, Howard, in camp on the east bank of the Salmon River, a mile and a half above the mouth of White Bird Creek, ran up an American flag over his command tent. Nez Percés, watching the troops to monitor their movement and potential threat, immediately raised their own red flag and invited the soldiers to cross the swollen river to fight.

The troops could not respond to the Nez Percé taunts. As Company H sergeant Michael McCarthy wrote, "Our force, except our company, were foot troops. A part of the next day was spent in trying to swim the Cavalry but it was a failure. A raft was tried but it was a failure also." The soldiers marveled at how the Indians had crossed with women and children when, as the sergeant noted, "We didn't seem to have engineering skill enough to devise ways and means to cross."

And so the soldiers remained on their side of the river and spent that evening in camp singing, telling stories, and writing letters to mothers, wives, and sweethearts, giving instructions should they die in battle.

Looking Glass remained camped at the forks of the Clearwater on the reservation lands he had occupied for some months and made no move to join his Indian allies. Some men from his village had participated in raids on white settlers, but the chief and his main body of warriors had not moved since returning from Tolo Lake at the beginning of the hostilities. All outward appearances indicated that Looking Glass would remain neutral in the conflict. Even so, Howard ordered Captain Stephen G. Whipple, a thirty-seven-year-old Vermonter who had fought Indians in California and Oregon, to "surprise and capture this chief and all that belonged to him."

This two-hundred-pound blue-eyed, black-haired, and bearded officer arrived at the Looking Glass camp on July 1 with two companies of cavalry. Whipple attempted to talk with the headman, but any possibility of peaceful surrender by Looking Glass went up with the smoke of a discharged military weapon that felled a tribesman. Soldiers then launched a full-scale attack on the village. Bullets ripped through the camp, tearing holes in lodges as the Nez Percés fled into bushes and trees and put up only a minimal defense. The soldiers captured Looking Glass's six hundred head of horses and cattle, looted the camp, smashed brass kettles, rode their horses through Indian gardens, and set at least two lodges on fire. When they withdrew they had neither arrested Looking Glass nor subdued his people, in spite of the near-crippling blow struck by capture of their horses. After the soldiers retreated, the Indians cautiously returned to their camp, hoping to salvage some possessions. One woman and her baby had drowned in the Clearwater as they attempted to flee the attack, and several other Nez Percés had been wounded or killed.

Joseph and those with him benefited from the unprovoked attack on Looking Glass and his people. The band that had heretofore stayed out of the conflict would soon join the nontreaty Nez Percés in wholehearted support, adding more fighting men to Joseph's cause. And the attack brought to the chiefs' council another experienced leader who had vast knowledge of fighting techniques, the lands of the Nez Percé, and the buffalo country to the east. Looking Glass would eventually provide primary war chief leadership for the Nez Percés.

On July 1, the day Whipple's command attacked Looking Glass, General Howard's troops finally crossed the Salmon River. Their success at being in the same area as Joseph and the non-treaty Nez Percés was short-lived, for as Joseph's cousin Yellow Wolf recalled, "Next morning scouts brought word the soldiers were on our side of the Salmon. This was good. We immediately crossed back to the north side." Howard's army rode in a cold rain and occasional snow, lost pack horses when they slipped on the wet grass and soil and rolled down steep hillsides, and became exasperated when they realized the river again stood between them and their quarry. "I know Joseph has crossed this God feared boiling caldron five times. . . . We can't cross it once," wrote Captain Robert Pollock of the Twenty-first Infantry.

"We crossed over the Salmon River, hoping General Howard would follow," Joseph said. "We were not disappointed. He did follow us, and we got between him and his supplies and cut him off for three days."

With Howard again held up by the river and separated from his supply lines, the Nez Percés intended to turn east, cross the broad, flat tableland of the Camas Prairie, and strike the Clearwater, but before they could make that move they learned of a troop of soldiers in camp at Norton's Ranch on Cottonwood Creek. Captain Whipple's men had arrived at Cottonwood on July 2, fresh from their attack on the Looking Glass band and with two Gatling guns in tow. These were ten-barreled hand-cranked .45 caliber weapons, drawn by three horses and attended by four-man teams. Whipple fortified his position at Cottonwood and sent out two scouts who located the Indians north of the creek. One scout rode back with the information, but the other was killed after his horse stumbled and fell. Whipple then ordered Lieutenant Sevier M. Rains, an 1876 West Point graduate, to ride north with ten men, telling him to keep to the high ground, which Rains failed to do. Nez Percé scouts watched Rains, commander of the First Cavalry's Company L, ride forward with five members of his own company and another five enlisted men from Company E. The Indians then moved in behind the cavalrymen, cut off their escape route, and attacked and killed Rains and the men with him.

Whipple and seventy soldiers approached the battle site and did not ride to Rains's aid but skirmished with the Indians before falling back to Cottonwood, where the captain sent a message to Howard: "Joseph with his entire force is in our front."

The general, stymied by the swirling Salmon, could not cross the river for another three days. Cut off from supply lines, his troops ran out of bacon and had to carve steaks off the horses killed in falling down ravines. During Howard's absence, the Nez Percés had killed Rains and his men, engaged Whipple, and then fought with seventeen Idaho volunteers on the Camas Prairie. Three of the civilians were killed and two wounded while Joseph's Nez Percés lost one warrior killed, their first battle death in the nearly three-week-old conflict.

Joseph and the others now moved rapidly to the east, driving some three thousand head of horses and cattle across the Camas Prairie to the South Fork of the Clearwater, where they regrouped and combined with the Looking Glass band. Together they had 225 warriors, about 75 armed only with bows and arrows, and another 600 old men, women, and children. The Indians set up a new camp west of the Clearwater, on the reservation lands defined for them by the 1863 Thief Treaty.

Defeated decisively at White Bird Canyon and again in the Cottonwood skirmishes, military troops and civilians reorganized and rode toward the Clearwater. On the night of July 8, a group of volunteers camped just a mile northwest of the Nez Percé village on the Clearwater. Ten men took up positions on a hillside near the Indian camp with instructions from their commander to send word if they saw Indians and to retain control of the hill even if attacked.

Two men crept to positions close to the Indian village, where they counted seventy-two lodges and twice that many horses tied or picketed around them. The men watched until day broke and the Indians began emerging from their lodges. The scouts returned to their own camp and sent a messenger to Howard telling him of their location and that of the Indians. The premature firing of a gun by one of the civilians alerted the Nez Percés, and they responded in force, causing all the volunteers to join their comrades on the hill piling rocks into breastworks to defend themselves. The location became known as Misery Hill after a daylong siege by warriors who captured forty-eight of the volunteers' horses, some of them animals that had been taken from Looking Glass days before. The tribesmen withdrew from their attack the evening of July 10 and the volunteers also abandoned their position.

Meantime, Howard's command, including civilians organized by Ad Chapman, the man who had fired the first shot at White Bird Canyon, who would become an interpreter for

Howard and remain with him throughout the conflict, took a route along a ridge above the Clearwater. The army contingent involved four companies of the First Cavalry with Captain David Perry in command and five companies of the Twenty-first Infantry under Captain Evan Miles, a Civil War veteran. These foot soldiers carried all their gear on their backs, including their rifles, forty to sixty rounds of ammunition, a wool blanket, poncho, tent canvas, mess utensils, food, canteen, and personal items.

Also in the force were five companies of the Fourth Artillery, similarly equipped, responsible for two twelve-pound howitzers and two Gatling guns, and commanded by Captain Marcus Miller. He had spent his entire career in the Fourth Artillery, seeing action during the Civil War at Richmond, Antietam, Fredericksburg, and Chancellorsville and later participating in the Modoc War of 1872–73, where he carried off a daring rescue of peace commissioners.

Ad Chapman spotted the Nez Percé village spread along the river valley a thousand feet below the army's position in an area with dense underbrush, a scattering of pine trees, and a steep hill rising behind it to the west. From this vantage point the army faced an equally steep, rocky descent to the river valley, where Indians were racing horses and swimming in the river, oblivious to the military on their doorstep.

It was near noon and the soldiers were moving into formation when the Indians spotted them. The Nez Percé women rushed out of the river, pulled on their long deerskin dresses, and returned to camp, where they began rounding up children and possessions. The men gathered horses and other stock, moving the animals up the Clearwater out of harm's way. Howard ordered one howitzer placed at the northeast end of the ridge, but the four-man crew found the village too distant for effective firing. Captain Miles then had the other howitzer and two Gatling guns moved farther south along the ridge, which placed them closer to the lodges.

The warriors organized into three main groups. Old Toolhoolhoolzote led twenty men up one ravine leading to the bluff while the other two groups remained near the camp to protect it. The Dreamer-led party successfully checked the advance of Howard's army, then some two miles long as it spread along the ridge.

When it became clear, because of the steep, rocky slope, that the soldiers could not immediately storm the village, other warriors, Joseph included, assaulted the various military positions, crawling up the hillside, darting behind brush and rocks for cover. They organized into small individual fighting units of two to four men who considered themselves warrior partners. First Cavalry sergeant Michael McCarthy of Company H took note of the Indians working in independent units. The native fighters rode horses to a vantage point, rolled to the ground, took aim and fired their weapons, and then remounted a horse that had stood quietly through the process.

The Indians concentrated on the howitzers, aware of their devastating power, and eventually overpowered the gunners, killing many of them.

As the battle continued, the Nez Percé sharpshooters also employed an unusual tactic by shooting at military officers, knowing if they injured or killed the leaders they could effectively throw the troops into chaos. As at White Bird Canyon, they also targeted buglers.

The battle eased as night fell, with many warriors retreating to protect the village. The fighting resumed on July 12 when Joseph and his fellow warriors again crept and crawled along the ravines and through the grass to within shooting range of the troops, while others made bold rushes at the enemy. "They tie grass upon their heads, so that it is hard to tell which bunch of grass does not conceal an Indian with a globe-sighted rifle," Lieutenant Melville Wilkinson of the Third Infantry later wrote in a letter to the *Army and Navy Journal*. The Indian sharpshooters kept up their fatal fusillade, striking one soldier in the head, another in the breast, and several in the buttocks, legs, and thighs. An officer, raising his arm to signal troops, had a bullet strike his wrist; another bullet pierced the neck of a canteen as a soldier tried to take a drink. The accurate shooting kept the soldiers from filling their canteens. "All day long under a hot July sun, without water and without food, our men crawled about in the parched grass, shooting and being shot at," said infantry lieutenant Charles Erskine Scott Wood of Erie, Pennsylvania, who served as Howard's aide-de-camp and secretary.

Late on July 12, the soldiers forged forward, forcing the Indians to retreat, although many warriors, unused to extended battles as this one had become, had already departed from the battleground, joining older men in the smoking lodge, an area protected by a rocky cliff and a rudely placed stone wall. Later, some Nez Percés claimed those warriors who withdrew did so out of cowardice, but it was known that an Indian could retreat from a battle at any time he believed his spiritual power no longer protected him. In some cases the fighters lit their pipes and smoked as a way to listen to or rekindle their spirit power. In any case, the reduction in Indian forces opposing the soldiers on the rocky ridgetop led to the collapse of their defenses.

As he saw the Indian lines might give way, Joseph halted

his own ridgeline attack on the soldiers, returned to the village, and told the camp that everyone must move quickly. Even with this warning, the sudden retreat by the Indians and the rush down the mountain by the military forces gave the women and children in camp little time to gather themselves and their possessions. Perhaps their inexperience in war had left the women unprepared for a direct assault on their camp even though they watched the two-day battle unfold before them. Now they fled, abandoning lodge poles, clothing, food, cattle herds, and cooking utensils. Joseph's cousin Yellow Wolf, with gunshot wounds below his left eye and to his left wrist, helped Joseph's wife Springtime, who was having trouble controlling her horse, and handed her the cradleboard holding her two-week-old baby girl as the people deserted the camp. The warriors raced their horses behind their escaping people and fired weapons at the oncoming troops.

That night Howard's troops camped within the abandoned Indian village, rummaging for buffalo robes, blankets, cooking utensils, and food, including salmon, dried meat, and coffee. They broke into food and storage caches, burned the goods, and donned buckskin clothing, beaded moccasins, and other Nez Percé paraphernalia.

Twelve soldiers died during the two-day battle and two more later died of wounds received; another twenty-three were wounded. Nearly half the casualties were officers, buglers, and noncommissioned officers.

At least four Nez Percé warriors died and another six were injured at the Clearwater, and their camp had been overtaken and destroyed. This was a serious setback for Joseph and the other headmen following the successful engagements at White Bird Canyon and Cottonwood. Now they moved toward a familiar camping place, the Weippe Prairie, where their forebears had met Lewis and Clark in peace in 1805 and where they had gathered camas bulbs for untold generations.

An aide of General McDowell's, with Howard on the battlefield at the Clearwater, sent a message to his superior: "Joseph is in full flight westward."

He was wrong.

The Lolo Trail Beckons

The Nez Percés regrouped near Kamiah, a subagency of the reservation where treaty Indians had culti-vated fields of new corn and wheat and operated a ferry over the Clearwater River. The anti-treaty tribesmen forded the river and then destroyed the Kamiah ferry to slow pursuit by the army they knew would follow them. East of the river they set up a new camp and built stone barricades for defense when the soldiers arrived.

General O. O. Howard had a decisive victory in his pocket but did not rapidly pursue the Indians after the Clearwater battle of July 11–12. When his troops reached Kamiah an ad-vance party came upon the destroyed ferry and sighted Joseph's people weaving among the Ponderosa pines, heading up a steep hillside, traveling north. Once again a river tem-porarily halted the general and his troops. Nez Percé riflemen hiding in the rocks, brush, and trees on their side of the river laid down a pattern of rifle fire that prevented the soldiers from fording the river and gave the Indian families time to

evade capture. Initially there was a short but intense fight between the two sides. Many warriors remained in the camp beside the Clearwater for two days as Howard's troops dug into
positions in the corn and wheat fields to the west.

As at the Salmon, the tribesmen taunted the soldiers; then
Lewiston volunteer Eugene T. Wilson watched as an Indian,
at that time believed by the troops to be Joseph but actually
the Wallowa Band member No Heart, "sauntered down to the
river's bank upon a mission of diplomacy." As he approached
the river he called across to the troops to say that the Indians
were ready to surrender. No Heart's action had been directed
by Joseph. It was common for a leader to send a trusted com-
rade on such a mission, as Joseph had sent Ollokot to meet
with Howard three months before at the Umatilla reservation.

General Howard, with several companies of the First Cavalry
and forty volunteers, marched south intending to ford the
Clearwater at a point twenty miles away, then flank the Nez
Percés. The remaining troops would remain at Kamiah, eventually cross the river there, and press the Indians from behind.
Howard believed this two-prong pressurized attack would
end the flight of the non-treaty bands. However, when his
force had marched about four miles south of Kamiah he received word that a Nez Percé representing Joseph wanted to
discuss surrender. The general immediately reversed his
troops and returned to Kamiah, where he met with No Heart.
The parley gave Howard the impression that Joseph was willing to halt the flight and return to the reservation under terms
the government dictated. Accordingly, Howard began efforts
to prepare for the unconditional surrender of the Nez Percés,

sending an optimistic message to his commander, General Irwin McDowell: "Joseph has promised to break away from White Bird and give himself up to-morrow. He said he was forced to move to-day."

Although his troops had been stymied by the Clearwater, Howard knew the Indians had been seriously hurt during the recent battle. "The indications are that they have but little ammunition or food, and sustained large losses of everything in their hurried crossing of the river here at our approach," he wrote McDowell. "I see evidence of the band's breaking up, and shall pursue them a little farther with vigor."

The following day, the troopers sweltered in their wool pants and shirts as the sun bore down while they waited for the parley their commander expected to have with Joseph. As the afternoon passed and Howard talked with No Heart, gunfire broke out from the opposite bank of the Clearwater signaling a halt to the discussion. The Lewiston volunteer, Eugene Wilson, said No Heart, whom he wrongly believed was Joseph himself, "slapped that portion of his anatomy which his leggins did not reach, and rode off."

Howard had lost the opportunity to outflank the Indians and was furious at what he considered a ruse engineered by Joseph to slow the army's advance. Now the Nez Percé families could head east over the Lolo Trail, a route traveled for decades as the tribe journeyed to the buffalo-hunting grounds of Montana.

Two days earlier, at the time Howard's troops took up positions on the west side of the Clearwater, the Indian families struck their camp beside the river and rode their horses up the steep hills toward Weippe Prairie. There the women prepared crude shelters made from brush wrapped with hide or mat lodge coverings. They had no lodge poles to set a proper tipi; that essential element of their homes had been left back at the village they had hastily abandoned on the Clearwater. With little food for their families, the women began harvesting camas, digging tender bulbs from the massive fields of the wild plant at Weippe Prairie and placing them in carrying bags and baskets woven from hemp. They did not have the time to properly roast and preserve this essential food item but would use it quickly, before it could spoil.

While the women replenished food supplies as best they could, headmen discussed their tactics. Joseph argued that the warriors should return to Kamiah and engage Howard's troops. He told the others he was not afraid to fight, an accusation made near Tolo Lake when the conflict first started. "What are we fighting for?" he said. "Is it for our lives? No. It is for this land where the bones of our fathers are buried. I do not want to take my women among strangers. I do not want to die in a strange land."

Looking Glass persuasively told the headmen they should turn east and cross the Lolo Trail into buffalo country. He knew the route and said the Nez Percés could find the Crows there and enlist aid from them, if necessary. The Crows would be friendly, Looking Glass argued, because some years before the Nez Percés had aided them during a fight with Lakotas, their hereditary enemies. Looking Glass had been assured the Crows would support the Nez Percés in any future conflicts; he did not take into account—perhaps did not know—that the Crows had backed the army in its battle with the Lakotas the previous year at Little Bighorn.

As the discussion continued, Joseph told the headmen, "Some of you tried to say, once, that I was afraid of the whites. Stay here with me now, and you shall have plenty of fighting." He suggested they leave the women, children, and elderly people in the mountains, then turn and engage the troops who had followed them. "Let us die on our own land fighting for them," he said. "I would rather do that than run I know not where." No doubt part of his reluctance to travel to the buffalo country centered on hardships he anticipated the families would have to endure on such a long trip and his own lack of knowledge about those lands and the route to them.

In the end, Looking Glass, older than Joseph and respected for war experience, won support from White Bird—who had initially advocated heading northeast into Canada—and the tribe's most powerful warriors, Rainbow and Five Wounds. The leadership of the combined bands now fell to Looking Glass, with Joseph assuming responsibility for the families and the horse herd, the key to their transportation and survival. Ollokot would continue his role as war leader of the young Wallowa Band fighters.

Though it is clear Joseph wanted to remain and fight for his land, he supported the others when the majority voted to proceed to the buffalo country, find the Crows, and seek sanctuary and assistance from them. During the course of these discussions, some Indians led by Red Heart, en route home from a buffalo-hunting trip, came into Joseph's camp. These Nez Percés had no stake in the conflict and after a visit proceeded west, where Howard promptly took them prisoner, parading them as "captives" to the journalists traveling with his army. The Lewiston, Idaho, *Teller* reported that Red

Heart's band included sixteen men and twenty-three women and children who had "their hair cut short." They were forced to cut their hair when they were taken captive. The newspaper displayed the commonplace frontier sentiment when it said that the cutting of the Indians' hair "should have been under the scalp." Red Heart's Indians, who had not been involved with Joseph's uprising and flight, were, nevertheless placed in irons and jailed for nine months as prisoners of war.

The non-treaty bands, augmented by two of Red Heart's sons who had elected to stay with Joseph, began their journey toward the buffalo country, following the Lolo Trail. This rough track had been upgraded in 1866 to make it a better route for commerce between the gold towns of Lewiston, Idaho, located eighty miles to the west, and Virginia City, Montana, a community in the southwest portion of that Territory. Virginia City had sprung up on the heels of the gold discovery at Alder Gulch in 1864 and soon replaced the earlier gold town of Bannack, located farther north and west, as the territorial capital of Montana.

The Lolo Trail traversed a rugged mountain range, and even with improvements it never became widely used by non-Indian travelers. Now, eleven years after the engineering changes, the Nez Percés found it overgrown with timber and brush. One soldier who followed it behind the Indians said the forest trail was so thick with standing and downed trees and underbrush that he couldn't throw a cat through it.

The Indians traveled on horseback with all of their possessions tied onto packhorses. Men and women had their own mounts. Mothers, such as Joseph's wife Springtime, hung their infant cradleboards over the pommel. Teenage boys herded the extra horses. Older children rode their own horses, sometimes in tandem with elders who were no longer strong enough to ride alone, while little ones were tied onto the tops of packs. The women led the packhorses through the forest, picking their way around granite boulders and downed timber. When they took breaks, the women dug for camas and other plant foods. In one place they found mussels; at streams they fished for trout and salmon. The horses grazed on wire grass and nibbled other edible plants, ignoring the lupine "loco weed" that would make them uncontrollable.

Upon leaving Weippe, the headmen had five warriors remain on the back trail, watching for Howard or his scouts. These men confronted three of the scouts, killing one and injuring two more, including Joseph's nephew James Reuben, the Lapwai interpreter. The general had already halted pursuit to allow additional troops to join up, and this action further delayed the army. By the time the Indians were nearly across the Bitterroot Mountains, they had a ten-day lead on Howard's force.

March to the Big Hole

Regular army troops established the Post at Missoula, the forerunner of a fort at Missoula, Montana, a week after the battle with the Nez Percés at White Bird Canyon. Creation of this post came in response to settler concerns in the Bitterroot Valley that Salish, or, as they were called, Flathead, Indians then being relocated onto a reservation northeast of Missoula would revolt following the Nez Percé example. Captain Charles C. Rawn, a forty-year-old Pennsylvanian of the Seventh Infantry, established the post.

After General Howard, then located at Kamiah, was certain that the Nez Percés were headed east, he split his command into three parts. With his forty-seven officers, 540 enlisted men, and seventy-four Indian scouts and civilians he would follow Joseph's direct trail. Traveling a route farther north into Montana was a party comprised of 440 enlisted men and thirty-six officers. A third complement of 245 enlisted men, twenty-two officers, and thirty-five Indian scouts would remain in the Salmon River country and at the Camas Prairie to protect settlers should the Indians circle back to that area. As Howard prepared to resume the pursuit, he sent a message to Captain Rawn at Missoula: "If you simply bother them and keep them back until I can close in, their destruction or surrender will be for sure."

Rawn called for volunteers to protect the Bitterroot Valley from incursion by the Nez Percés, and with 150 settlers, five officers, thirty enlisted men, and fifteen Flathead Indians to serve as interpreters he marched west. His goal was a narrow spot on the Lolo Trail, the only flat portion of the route, and one where he believed he could halt the Indians as Howard wanted. Once they arrived at their defensive position, the volunteers and soldiers set to work digging rifle pits and throwing up a log barricade to block the route. As they worked, the Flatheads with Rawn tied white cloths around their arms to identify them as allies of the troops and volunteers should fighting occur.

The Nez Percés, already crossing the Lolo Trail and bound for the buffalo country, sent a runner to the Salish, their longtime allies, who lived north of Missoula, but Chief Charlo refused to join them, a decision that denied the Nez Percés the option to travel toward Canada as White Bird had advocated. Initially Charlo pledged neutrality in the conflict, but he soon sided with the army, providing the military intelligence on the location of the Nez Percés and sending some of his men with Captain Rawn to the canyon barricade. There Charlo himself joined the soldiers before the Nez Percés reached that location.

When runners who had met with the Salish chief brought back the news of his refusal to join the Nez Percés, they also told Joseph and the headmen of the troops blocking the trail ahead. Nearing the blockaded site, the headmen left the women and children at a camp a dozen miles back on the trail while they pushed forward and opened talks with Rawn. The captain met with Joseph, Looking Glass, and White Bird on July 27. The Indian leaders said they wished to make a peaceful trip through the Bitterroot Valley on their way to the buffalo country and the Crow territory in Montana.

"I refused to allow them to pass unless they complied with my stipulations as to the surrender of their arms," Rawn wrote three days later.

The Indians told Rawn, "We are going by you without fighting if you will let us, but we are going by you anyhow." Joseph and Looking Glass told the captain they would travel through the Bitterroot Valley without harming anyone living there if allowed to pass the captain and his troops without a fight. Rawn refused such terms, but the much larger force of Montana volunteers, who recognized that any fight in the canyon might spill down the east flank of the Bitterroot and affect their own families in the valley below, agreed not to oppose the Nez Percés. The civilians began withdrawing from the barricaded area, returning to their homes, trusting that Looking Glass and Joseph would not renege on their promise.

Rawn, greatly outnumbered now that most of the volunteers had withdrawn, settled in with his troops for a tense night made more uncomfortable when it began to rain. The soldiers had dug a few rifle pits, but most of the troops were stationed behind the log barricade, constructed with loopholes through which they could fire their weapons. The greater concern was their location in the canyon. The soldiers, whose fortifications were on the floor of the canyon, realized the Indians could move onto the hillsides above them and shoot down upon their positions.

After most of the Montana men withdrew, the Nez Percé families resumed their journey. Volunteer Wilson Harlan, from his picket post on the mountain above the barricade, sent a message to Rawn during the night as he saw the Indians climb the ridge. "A fourth of a mile above our camp. . . . I saw squaws and children with camp stuff going up," Harlan said. He watched the Indian families avoid the canyon and instead travel across the high ground, riding their horses through the steady rain that softened the sound of their passage. The route became slick as they descended one steep hillside, then climbed another and rode behind the ridge, skirting around Rawn's troops and his barricaded location, soon known as "Fort Fizzle." As the Indian families moved through the night, some warriors fired a few rounds toward the soldiers, creating a diversion so their families could get by Rawn's troops, many of whom were too badly frightened to answer the fire.

Once around the army barricade, the Nez Percés dropped into the Bitterroot Valley and turned south. The headmen had instructed their people to cause no trouble in Montana, and by passing peacefully through that area they believed they would leave their trouble behind in Idaho. They moved at a moderate pace, taking time to buy or trade for supplies from settlers and merchants as they followed the Bitterroot River. In no case during those early days in Montana did they take anything without paying for it. They believed they would be allowed to ride peacefully across the country just as they had often done when heading into buffalo lands.

On July 30, 1877, a group of Nez Percé women accompanied by armed warriors appeared at the Buck Brothers store in Stevensville, just south of the point where the Lolo Trail emerged from the mountains and about thirty miles from the military's Post at Missoula. The women sought to purchase flour and other supplies. Henry Buck later wrote that he had no flour to trade, but the Indians obtained some from a nearby mill. He sold other items to the Indians, who paid him with gold coins. The following day a larger party of warriors, accompanied by White Bird, arrived in Stevensville.

"They were all well dressed with apparently new showy blankets, well armed, and rode the finest of horses," Buck said. "The Nez Percés were by far the finest-looking tribe of Indians I have ever seen. We had always considered the Nez Percés as a wealthy tribe and on this visit they seemed to have plenty of money, all in gold coin." Some of the younger warriors obtained whiskey in Stevensville and settlers feared for their safety, but before they could cause any trouble White Bird ordered them back to the main camp.

Buck watched as the entire band of Nez Percés then rode south following the Bitterroot River upstream. "As was always customary with Indians traveling on horseback, they jogged their ponies along on a little dog trot," he wrote. The merchant took out his pocket watch and timed their passing. "It took just one hour and a quarter for all to move by and there were no gaps in the continuous train," he said.

With flour and other supplies, including new blankets and shirts needed to replace items lost in the battle at the Clearwater, the Nez Percés traveled about fourteen miles a day, following the Bitterroot to its forks. They then took the east branch into Ross's Hole, where they left the Bitterroot, crossed the Continental Divide, and dropped into the next drainage. This, a long-known camping place called the Place of the Ground Squirrels, lay beside a clear, winding river with a timbered hill to the northwest and a great open valley to the south. The Nez Percés also knew it as the Big Hole.

There they laid out a proper village, intending to cut new lodge poles to replace the ones left at the Clearwater. Women prepared cooking pits, and with the North Fork of the Big Hole River running clear and swift beside their camp the people bathed and children ran races and played games, while the men hunted for fresh game to feed their families. These were the first relaxed moments they had allowed themselves in six weeks. "No more fighting!" Yellow Wolf said. "We had left General Howard and his war in Idaho."

Other Indians had joined them as they moved down the Bitterroot Valley, including Lean Elk, a man known to the whites as Poker Joe, who brought with him members of his family and others, adding a dozen lodges to the Nez Percé camp. This short man with a booming voice was Nez Percé and French-Canadian. He knew the country ahead and joined the headmen in setting the course for travel.

After the Nez Percés skirted the army's barricade on the Lolo Trail, Captain Rawn withdrew to the Post at Missoula to be joined there by Colonel John Gibbon, commander of the District of Montana. Gibbon, of Holmesburg, Pennyslvania, was a West Pointer who fought in the Mexican War, in the removal of the Seminole Indians from Florida in 1853, and at Fredericksburg and Gettysburg during the Civil War. He had served at a number of western forts before commanding the Montana Column in 1876 during the Little Bighorn battle. In the course of his Civil War service he sustained serious wounds, and in the Indian fighting on the Northern Plains he became known as One Who Limps.

By the summer of 1877, Gibbon commanded both the District of Montana and Fort Shaw on the Sun River in Montana. In order to take part in the Nez Percé troubles, his command marched 150 miles from Shaw to the Post at Missoula in just seven days, using pack mules to haul supplies. At Missoula, Gibbon combined his force with troops under Rawn's command and other companies, and on August 4, 1877, he set off with this combined force of seventeen officers and 145 enlisted men, plus thirty-four volunteers, trailing the Nez Percés south through the Bitterroot Valley. His army was just four days behind the Indian families and Gibbon pushed his soldiers to make double marches in his effort to catch up.

At Ross's Hole, three days and eighty miles south of Missoula, Gibbon realized the Indians had entered the mountains south of the Bitterroot and would soon be in the Big Hole Valley. When volunteers traveling with him wanted to quit the pursuit, Gibbon assured them he would find the Nez Percés and strike "a terrible blow."

On the night of August 7, two of Gibbon's lieutenants took fifty soldiers and volunteers and moved ahead of the main column, hoping to find the Nez Percé village, stampede the horses, and halt their journey. The reconnaissance party did not find the camp that first night, and at daylight the men took shelter in a ravine while the two lieutenants proceeded ahead until they heard the sound of axes—the Nez Percé women cutting lodge poles. The officers climbed trees and spied on the working women and from their perches saw the Indian camp beside the Big Hole River.

The Indians relaxed at the Big Hole, believing they had out-run the army. Women prepared the new lodge poles, cooked meals from freshly killed game, and, in a lodge separate from the main village, one gave birth. The men dressed in their finest garments to participate in a warrior parade, and Joseph, now battle tested, wore buckskin leggings, moccasins, and a waist-length red coat decorated with ermine tails attached like a fringe to the shoulders and sleeves and accented with blue beads, brass rivets, and small circles of navy blue material.*

As they made their way to the camp, White Bird and Lean Elk had cautioned Looking Glass that the soldiers might yet follow and that they should speed up their pace.

Lone Bird spoke of a dream he had: "My shaking heart tells me trouble and death will overtake us if we make no hurry through this land." Shore Crossing, the young warrior who with his friend Red Moccasin Tops had killed the first settlers in the Salmon River Valley, setting off the string of events that brought the Nez Percés to this place, also had a premonition of danger. He told the headman of his dream in which he saw himself and others being killed. He and Red Moccasin Tops offered to ride back over their trail to be cer-

---

*This coat is now among the artifacts displayed at the Big Hole Bat-tlefield visitor's center in Nez Percé National Historical Park near Wis-dom, Montana.

tain no soldiers followed, but they needed to borrow fast horses from a wealthy Nez Percé to make such a journey. That man refused the use of his horses, and Looking Glass, who did not see the risk of further attack, did not post scouts on their back trail or set any pickets to watch the camp at night.

Following their warrior parade, singing, drumming, and contests of both luck and skill, it was near midnight on August 8 when the camp finally quieted. Many of the men slept outside in the tall grass beside the river, but the families rolled into blankets and robes inside their lodges. Joseph joined his wives and children in their lodge near the riverbank on the northwest side of the village. He had worn his bright red chief's coat for the warrior parade. This fine garment now lay beside his sleeping place.

The Nez Percés had bypassed Captain Rawn and were already trading for supplies in the Bitterroot Valley by the time General Howard departed his camp at Kamiah and began pursuit of the non-treaty bands. Howard's troops struck the 100-mile-long Lolo Trail on Monday, July 30. It was raining and, forced to travel in single file because of the narrowness of the path, they slogged through "one of the most slippery, sticky, mucky and filthy" days they had endured, according to a report in the *New York Herald.* Over the next week Howard's army tackled harsh terrain marked by fallen trees, bog holes, rocks, steep hillsides, and sparse grass for their animals, since it had been clipped short by the nearly 3,000 Nez Percé horses.

A group of frontiersmen, called Skillets by the soldiers, traveled ahead of Howard, working to improve the route.

These men were organized as an engineering and infantry unit and were commanded by forty-one-year-old Twenty-first Infantry captain William F. Spurgin, who served in the Civil War with a unit from Indiana and under Howard in the post–Civil War Freedmen's Bureau. Cavalrymen each carried ten pounds of grain for their horses but often resorted to feeding the animals bark stripped from trees. The men had short rations, too, which they occasionally supplemented with fish from the clear mountain streams they crossed.

At the four hot springs near Lolo, the troops eased sore bodies by bathing in the hot water. While there, Howard learned that Colonel Gibbon had begun his own pursuit of the Nez Percés and even then was headed up the Bitterroot Valley. Howard wrote Gibbon on August 6 instructing him, as he had earlier told Captain Rawn, to "create delay by skirmishing, by parleying, or maneuvering in any way, so that they shall not get away from you." Howard said he would proceed as rapidly as possible with two hundred cavalrymen.

Gibbon led his command out of Ross's Hole and toward the divide separating the Bitterroot and Big Hole rivers at dawn on August 8. The route was steep and treacherous, with rocks and downed trees blocking the path. Teamsters with the supply wagons, who could travel three or four miles an hour on easier terrain, found themselves struggling to make a few hundred yards in an hour. Double teams were required to pull each wagon up the rough road to where the mules were unhitched and headed back down the trail to be rehitched to another wagon. This backbreaking work exhausted both men and animals, and as the day progressed the mules that had played out under the strain were abandoned by the trail. In some places infantrymen used picks and shovels to improve crossings for the wagons, but despite this labor, it took six hours to move less than three miles.

By late afternoon the wagons reached the ravine where the advance party had halted upon approaching the Indian camp. That night Gibbon ordered silence in his bivouac and allowed no campfires. The men chewed a bit of uncooked bacon and hardtack for their evening meal, then rested until near midnight, when Gibbon aroused himself from his sleep and ordered the command forward. The soldiers discarded overcoats and some even left behind their canteens as they passed quietly through the dark pine and fir forest, waded a cold mountain creek, and crossed a boggy area with only the light of the stars to guide them.

Before dawn on August 9, the army had moved within sight of the Nez Percé camp and its eighty-nine lodges. All was peaceful. No sentry stood; a few dogs foraged for something to eat or barked at coyotes that had crept close to the village. The soldiers spread out along a hillside to the northwest of the camp, intending to form a crescent-like line that would separate the Nez Percés from their horses and force the Indians to the south onto the open, rolling prairie of the Big Hole Valley.

The troopers were nearly in place for the attack when an old Indian with failing eyesight moved from the camp to check his horses. He came upon the waiting soldiers but could not identify them in the dim light. Gibbon's men realized they had lost their element of surprise. Shots rang out, the Indian fell, and the order "Go in and strike them hard" came from an officer as the soldiers poured a volley of gunfire into the camp. Black powder smoke drifted up obscuring the misty dawn and the Nez Percé village awoke in a confusion that quickly turned to pandemonium.

Joseph pulled a deerskin shirt over his head when the first gunshots rang out. Children and women stumbled from beneath blankets and buffalo robes as bullets smacked the lodges like hailstones or a hard rain. The people hugged the ground seeking protection from Mother Earth herself. Bullets struck both of Joseph's wives. He grabbed his baby daughter and ran from the lodge, turned toward the river, and sought shelter in tall grass.

Other women shepherded youngsters toward the river, too; some crouched in the grass or dove into the water to find protection from the incessant volleys of rifle fire.

Two Moons hugged the ground with his family in their lodge during the initial wave of bullets. When the shooting subsided, he retrieved his gun and took cover in tall grass near the river as bullets sputtered around him like "acorns in the autumn winds." Soldiers passed his refuge, one on a horse that came so close it almost stepped on him. After the men had passed, he met Joseph, unarmed and carrying the baby. Two Moons told him to run: "Without the gun you can do nothing! Save the child!"

In the confusion of the dawn raid, many warriors, like Joseph, found themselves unarmed and had to crouch in the tall grass beside the river. Some men had their war horses tethered close to their lodges, but most of the animals were killed in the opening volleys of gunfire. Not all of Joseph's people found places to hide. Wave after wave of gunfire raked the village and the tall grass beside the river. Adults, children, babies, were mowed down in the curtain of bullets; the river ran with the blood of those killed there; old men and women wailed and keened.

With little resistance, Gibbon's soldiers entered the camp, cut holes in the hide and mat lodge coverings, and then set them on fire, burning alive the elderly and children, who would not leave their injured or dead kin. Other women and children fled the burning structures and were shot down. In the maternity lodge, soldiers killed the new mother and the older woman who had attended her, before they crushed the skull of the hours-old infant.

Teenage boys, responsible for guiding the horse herd as the people traveled, raced toward the animals that had moved away from the camp and the constant gunfire. Joseph was with the horses. He had handed the baby to a woman for safekeeping, joined No Heart, and the two mounted quickly and began driving the herd up the hill, away from the fighting, but in the confusion of the morning a Nez Percé shot and killed No Heart, believing him to be a Flathead working with the American troops. This left Joseph to herd the horses alone until the younger boys arrived.

In the chaotic village, meantime, White Bird took charge of the defense, commanding the men to protect their families. Looking Glass also rallied the Indian fighters as he called to Shore Crossing and Red Moccasin Tops to show their courage. Warriors blew their eagle-bone whistles, said to draw power and the assistance of their spirit helpers.

As the camp defenders regrouped and followed the directions of White Bird and Looking Glass to counter-attack, the battle quickly turned to hand-to-hand fighting. Ollokot, with one of his wives injured in the battle, fought beside the other young men, many armed with only battle-axes or bows. Few of the Nez Percé fighters had guns and ammunition when the battle erupted but retrieved carbines, bayonets, and cartridge belts from fallen troopers, some of whose corpses floated in the Big Hole River beside their Indian victims.

The lieutenant who had been leading men intent on capturing and stampeding the Indian horses was killed in a volley of Indian fire, and his unorganized men retreated to support their comrades in the middle of the line. Nez Percé sharpshooters positioned themselves in trees and began targeting military commanders, including Colonel Gibbon, whose horse fell to a bullet that passed through the commander's thigh.

The bravest Indian fighters hit the soldiers head-on. Shore Crossing hid in a slight depression in the ground and crouched behind a single rotten log, killing and wounding several soldiers before a bullet struck him in the head. His pregnant wife, already wounded in the attack, picked up the carbine and shot the man who had killed her husband, then fell to the soldiers' bullets. She is the only Nez Percé woman known to have fired a gun at the attackers in the battle.

White Bird's counter-attack drove the soldiers back from the camp toward a timbered point as the early-morning battle dragged into midday. "It soon became evident that the enemy's sharp-shooters, hidden behind trees, rocks, &c, possessed an immense advantage over us, in so much that we could not compete with them," Gibbon later wrote. "At almost every crack of a rifle from the distant hills some member of the command was sure to fall."

With the troops entrenched on the hillside farther away from the camp, Joseph brought the horses back to the village where he and others wept at the sight of men, women, elders, children, and babies lying there dead among burned lodges and smoking buffalo robes. When he told the people they must prepare to move quickly, even the warriors sometimes broke away from the attack to bury a family member or care for a wounded wife or child. Joseph, with his own two wives injured, helped pack their camp goods.

Bitterroot settler and volunteer soldier Tom Sherrill, with the soldiers on the hillside, later wrote: "I noticed from my position the camp of Joseph; the squaws and papooses were busy gathering up the camp outfit, buffalo robes, blankets and saddles and saddling the horses and packing them. They were tying wounded Indians to them."

Under Joseph's direction and with White Bird's assistance, the Nez Percés set off south into the Big Hole Valley. The new lodge poles they had just cut were covered with hides and lashed to horses as travois to transport the people most severely wounded. Many warriors accompanied the retreating bands to care for injured wives and children; others joined their families to protect them against further attack. In their camp they left behind hastily dug shallow graves, abandoned pans, ovens, pots, riding and pack saddles, and buffalo robes; many of their lodge coverings had been burned or ruined. Scattered about were dead or crippled horses and dead dogs.

With the remains of their families now on the move south, one party of warriors led by Ollokot stayed at the camp beside the Big Hole River to restrain the soldiers and delay any pursuit. They captured a howitzer that Gibbon's men intended to use against them, eventually dismantling and burying the big gun. They set the grass on fire so flames licked toward the west where the soldiers had entrenched. They cut ropes holding a pack on one of the army horses, finding more than 2,000 rounds of ammunition, and picked up as many soldier rifles as they could carry.

The Indians chose not to attack the soldiers in their hastily established fortifications, this for good reason: "If we killed one soldier, a thousand would take his place," Yellow Wolf said. "If we lost one warrior, there was none to take his place."

At the Big Hole battle the Nez Percés had lost dozens of warriors killed, including Shore Crossing, Red Moccasin Tops, Rainbow, and Five Wounds, among the best of their fighting men. Adding the women and children, Gibbon's troops had killed more than eighty of the non-treaty Indians in that early-morning battle but had failed to capture the horse herd, and as a result the Indians, suffering terribly from their losses, were again on the run.

Bitterroot Valley volunteer Tom Sherrill* called that August 9, 1877, "rather a sad and exciting day."

During that day of carnage, the Nez Percé fighters made three efforts, the final one successful, to retrieve the body of Red Moccasin Tops. They did not want his corpse to fall into enemy hands and sought the wolf pelt—his spirit helper—he carried, believing it would continue to provide power to the People. The warriors commanded by Ollokot harassed the soldiers through the night. Gibbon and many of his troops

---

* When the Big Hole Battlefield was first set aside as a protected area, Sherrill became its first manager.

were wounded and suffered from lack of water, food, and medical attention. Ollokot's warriors broke away from the fight on August 10 when a courier Howard had sent arrived at Gibbon's position. Now they would watch their back trail; they would heed warnings brought to them in dreams by spirit helpers; they would travel more quickly.

Looking Glass no longer commanded the non-treaty bands. In the aftermath of the fight at the Big Hole, Lean Elk, knowing the way to the buffalo country, took over as leader of the bands and Joseph embraced his position as camp chief and protector of the families.

General Howard missed the action at the Big Hole but provided support in the aftermath. Twenty-five soldiers and six volunteers died at the Big Hole and another thirty-eight men were wounded. Once again the Indians, superior marksmen, had targeted officers and buglers to disrupt military command. Gibbon had no medical team with his command, but Howard's field surgeons treated some of those who were injured and sent the others toward the Post at Missoula. They were transported in rough army wagons over the trail so laboriously crossed just days before. Howard's men helped bury Gibbon's dead troopers and volunteers.

Gibbon, suffering from the wound to his thigh, could not continue in the field against the Nez Percés, so Howard again assumed full command and set out to follow the clear trail the Nez Percés had taken.

With an Eye Toward the Buffalo Country

T he bodies of dead and dying Nez Percés marked the trail from the Big Hole. Fearful that the soldiers would soon follow, Joseph and White Bird set a steady course, halting only long enough to bury the dead, including one of Ollokot's wives, Fair Land, a woman who left behind a baby. Some elder tribal members who had been injured chose to be abandoned so as not to delay the others.

The trail wound south and into another river valley in western Montana known as Horse Prairie, so called from its history as the area where Meriwether Lewis and William Clark had first negotiated for horses with the Shoshones in 1805. When the warriors who had remained with Ollokot at the Big Hole rejoined Joseph, Lean Elk assumed primary leadership, determining their route and manner of traveling. Almost immediately the Indians began a routine that kept them on the accelerated pace Joseph had set upon leaving the Big Hole. They rose early, traveled until mid-morning, halted to prepare a meal and allow their horses to graze; in midafternoon they resumed their march, traveling until late in the evening, then setting up a meager camp.

Now, even more so than after their fight at the Clearwater in mid-July, they had few possessions. Lodge coverings had been burned or otherwise destroyed at the Big Hole and they had left most of their camp goods behind, as well. In traveling through the Bitterroot Valley, the Nez Percés had carefully avoided making any hostile moves. They traded for or bought supplies they needed from merchants who then joined in the attack on their village. This incensed the young warriors and they sought revenge. Now, to replenish goods, they raided settlers and stole horses so that volunteers and soldiers would not find any mounts to use in pursuit. In some of the raids in southwest Montana, small bands of warriors killed white residents.

Lean Elk steered the Nez Percés away from Bannack City, a western Montana gold rush town that had been the first territorial capital, and angled the route to cross the Bitterroots at Bannock Pass. Once over that nearly treeless divide, the People were back into Idaho Territory, but rather than turning west toward their country, they followed the broad Lemhi Valley, skirting along the Idaho and Montana border. Along their easterly route, they raided for horses and supplies, fought limited engagements with residents, and in one place attacked freighters with eight wagons, killed most of them, and plundered their cargo. The Nez Percés met no military resistance as they marched down the Lemhi Valley, but it was coming.

It took three days for his support troops to join General Howard after his August 10 arrival at the Big Hole. He then added soldiers from Colonel John Gibbon's command and set out on Joseph's trail. After the Indians veered from a direct route to the buffalo country and crossed back into Idaho, Howard turned toward Bannack City, where, as newspaper correspondent Thomas Sutherland of the Portland *Daily Standard* wrote, "the entire town [turned] out in holiday attire." There the general recruited volunteers and planned a route that he believed would put him ahead of the Nez Percés and cut off their escape. As an added measure of security, he sent a company of cavalrymen farther east to wait for the Indians near Yellowstone National Park.

With new volunteers Howard followed the stage road south from Bannack City until scouts brought word that Joseph's camp was nearby. He considered pushing on into the night, but cavalry officers told him both horses and men were exhausted, so he reluctantly ordered them into bivouac. At dawn the march resumed, "with the infantry and Artillery hurrying after us, in country wagons, about a day behind," *Daily Standard* correspondent Sutherland said. Bitterroot Valley merchant Henry Buck, who had sold supplies to the Indians two weeks earlier, now drove one of those wagons used to pick up any footsore or exhausted soldiers. "I usually started out empty, but by camp time . . . I would have all the men that could get into the wagon," he said.

On August 19, the advance troops reached Camas Meadows in northeastern Idaho expecting to find Joseph's camp, but as Sutherland put it, "the birds had flown." Howard halted on a rocky knoll near two creeks and with plenty of grass nearby for the horses and mules.

Nine days passed before Joseph's people covered the nearly 200 miles from the Big Hole Valley to Camas Meadows, an area known to some Nez Percés who had made earlier trips to the region. They learned from scouts, who now remained vigilant, that Howard had nearly caught up to them and was in fact close to the camp they had made the previous night. But rather than taking flight as they had done before, the headmen took the offensive, inspired by the dream of the warrior Black Hair, who saw Indians, under cover of darkness, entering the soldiers' camp and taking their horses.

On the night of August 19, more than two dozen Nez Percé warriors led by Ollokot, Looking Glass, and Toolhoolhoolzote in full warrior garb—having tied their horses' tails up by twisting the hair into a knot or using a buckskin thong so the animals could run unimpeded—rode from the Indian encampment. They had devised a bold plan to slip into Howard's camp after dark, release the horse herd, and escape, taking the animals with them. Joseph supported the raid and went partway with the warriors but did not enter the army's bivouac.

In Howard's position, the soldiers hobbled the mares kept with the pack mules. These horses wore bells around their necks so sentries could hear their movements through the night, and since pack mules bonded with the bell mares, they would not stray far from them. Mules used to pull the supply wagons were tied to the wagon wheels. The men attached the cavalry horses securely to ropes stretched taut between picket pins and then settled in for the night.

The Indians rode stealthily toward Howard's camp, stopping only to discuss whether to enter the bivouac on foot or
horseback. Looking Glass wanted to remain mounted; warriors Two Moons and Wottolen argued they would be quieter
on foot and could kill the general and his top staff by attack-
ing them in their beds before taking the army horse herd.
Wottolen recalled, "Chief Looking Glass who generally opposed plans not his own," insisted on riding on horseback.
However, Looking Glass agreed that the younger men could
creep among the soldiers on foot and cut loose the army animals as Black Hair had seen in his dream. The decision ultimately came with Ollokot's order: "Breaking morning is
coming. Let us go!"

The army encampment came alive "by sharp firing and the di-
abolical yelling of Indians, about two hundred yards from the
headquarters tents," Portland reporter Thomas Sutherland
said. "We all ran out as quickly as possible, but as it was dark,
and as the volunteers had pitched tents across the creek from
the main command, in the immediate vicinity of the firing
and war-whoops, our guns were almost useless."

Sutherland could see enough to know the horse herd was
under attack. "Sweeping around our camp could be distin-
guished a herd of stampeded horses and mules, galloping at
their highest possible speed, with a considerable band of Indians behind goading them on with loud cries, and discharge
of rifles," he said.

The Indians never reached Howard's tent, nor did they release all of the military horses. One of the Nez Percés fired a
gun just as the raid began, alerting the camp. Nevertheless,

they captured nearly 150 animals and raced from the area. "The stampeded horses gone, we do not stay to fight soldiers," Wottolen said. "We leave them firing like crazy people in the darkness."

As they rode toward Joseph's position, the Indians found the pace of the animals slower than they had expected and at full daylight realized why. "We have only mules!" Wottolen said. The raiders had captured some horses belonging to Howard's volunteers and nearly all of the pack mules needed to carry troop supplies. The mules were not valued by the Indians but represented a serious loss to Howard, whose troubles at Camas Meadows had not yet ended.

The Nez Percés split their party after their raid. Some, including men who had been waiting in reserve for just such a purpose, took the mules and horses toward their own camp; others prepared to engage the cavalry, now organized and in pursuit. Camas Meadows was open, sagebrush country with few trees and limited opportunity for defensive actions, but the Indians positioned themselves behind a small rise in the basaltic ground. The three cavalry companies riding toward the Nez Percés and the stolen animals became disorganized. A sergeant later said the orderly gallop soon became a full-fledged horse race as cavalrymen had difficulty controlling their excited animals.

Second Cavalry captain Randolph Norwood, a Maryland native who had seen action in the Shenandoah Valley with the Maryland volunteer cavalry during the Civil War, rode in the center of the three cavalry units that had set out after the Indians. His Company L came face-to-face with the warriors as his men topped a ridge beyond which the Indians had stopped to await the soldiers. As with all cavalry units, the men worked in groups of four: three men handing over their horses to a fourth man responsible for holding his comrades' mounts while they fought afoot. Soon, thirty-five cavalrymen were on the ground ready to face the Nez Percés while the horse handlers retreated to a cottonwood grove about five hundred yards behind the skirmish line. The Indians over the rise were about one thousand yards away, standing behind their horses. For the first twenty or so minutes the two sides traded gunshots with "little damage on either side, as the range was long for our Springfields and longer for their Winchesters," said Second Cavalry sergeant Harry J. Davis, who was with Norwood's force.

While the soldiers concentrated on the Indians facing them, however, the Nez Percés "engineered as neat a double flank movement as could be imagined," Davis said, leaving the cavalrymen "exposed to a raking fire coming from right and left."

From the cottonwood thicket came the sound of Bernard Brooks's bugle as he played "Recall." Sergeant Davis said, "The race to that thicket was never to be forgotten, for a cavalryman is not trained for a five hundred yard sprint." Davis carried a horse's nose bag filled with extra cartridges, and as he ran toward the cottonwoods "a bullet cut the strap and let it fall to the ground. A hero would have stopped, gone back and recovered that bag, but not I," the sergeant said.

From his position in front of the skirmish line of cavalrymen, Wottolen said, "those soldiers run like deer for the shelter brush."

All of the soldiers, even those who had been wounded by the earliest shooting, made it back to the cottonwood grove, but an Indian sharpshooter shot and killed bugler Brooks.

The cavalrymen hid in a depression in the prairie where they had a few cottonwood trees in full leaf to provide shade and cover and here stacked lava rocks into twenty-three crude breastworks that encircled their position. The Nez Percés now surrounded the soldiers, sniping at them for two hours before retreating.

The First Cavalry companies that rode forward with Norwood's Second Cavalry troopers did not aid the besieged soldiers in the cottonwood grove; instead, they retreated to Howard's location at the first bugle call and after they joined Howard realized the third troop had not made it back.

The Indians withdrew and Howard sent men out to find Norwood, but it is unclear whether the additional troops caused the Nez Percés to quit the fight or they simply realized they could not dislodge Norwood from his sheltered area. Later the *New York Herald,* obviously sympathetic to the soldiers, reported: "It must be admitted that Joseph worsted us."

Norwood had been with Howard's command only one day when the fight occurred at Camas Meadows. From the Cantonment on Tongue River in eastern Montana he had escorted United States Army Commanding General William Tecumseh Sherman to Fort Ellis on the East Gallatin River three miles from Bozeman, Montana. There General Sherman, who was taking a small party to tour Yellowstone National Park, ordered Norwood and fifty-nine men to join Howard and assist in bringing the Nez Percés to heel. Howard, no longer in the military region he commanded, had been instructed by Sherman to disregard departmental boundaries and continue his pursuit of Joseph and the Nez Percés.

After the mule raid at Camas Meadows, Howard's army,

with no pack train to transport supplies, could not move forward. Therefore, he retreated to Virginia City, Montana, where he said he "bought nearly everything that the village could furnish in the way of provisions, clothing, and fresh animals."

Howard sent messages from Virginia City to General Irwin McDowell, his immediate superior in San Francisco, and to General Sherman, telling them his men and horses were worn out and suggesting it made more sense for fresh troops from other military departments to take up the pursuit.

"My command is so much worn by over fatigue and jaded animals that I cannot push it much further," he wrote to Sherman, then at Fort Shaw in central Montana on a tour of western forts. Sherman replied the same day telling Howard to "pursue the Nez Percés to the death, lead where they may." Other troops were too far distant to be of help, Sherman wrote, and added impatiently and, to a general officer, ominously: "If you are tired, give the command to some young, energetic officer."

Nothing could have stirred Howard's ire more quickly than the suggestion that he was too old and weary for continued pursuit. "You misunderstood me. I never flag," he replied. "You need not fear for the campaign. Neither you nor General McDowell can doubt my pluck and energy." Satisfied with his response, he set off from Virginia City with animals he had been assured were "well broken." He quickly found the assurances were lies. "The bucking of a half-broken half-breed pony is always exciting and frequently dangerous," he said. "Such a pitching and plunging, hooting and yelling, running and falling, made one think of danger ahead from something besides Indians."

Since Howard's advance had been slowed by the capture of the pack mules he needed to transport supplies, Joseph and the Nez Percés traveled around Henry's Lake toward Targhee Pass. The general had sent cavalry troops to that area to wait for the Indians, but this attempt to halt their forward movement failed. The troops withdrew before Joseph reached the pass, leaving the way open for him to cross the Continental Divide for the third time without conflict.

Once over the divide and back in Montana, the Nez Percés made an unanticipated move. They struck the Madison River on August 22 and turned east into Yellowstone National Park, something Sherman had predicted they would not do.

Yellowstone Interlude

That Montana summer of 1877 was particularly hot and dry, the weather contributing to a grasshopper plague. The insects irritated twenty-three-year-old Emma Cowan as they invaded her house in Radersburg, in central Montana near Helena, so when her husband, George, a prominent attorney and former United States marshal, suggested a vacation to Yellowstone National Park she readily agreed. The Park had been established just five years earlier but had already attracted hundreds of visitors eager to see geysers, boiling springs, bubbling mudpots, and wildlife. Emma invited her thirteen-year-old sister, Ida Carpenter, and brother, Frank, age twenty-seven, and her husband and brother asked five other men to accompany the party.

They had horses, a double-seated carriage, and a baggage wagon to haul food and other supplies and on August 9 reached the Madison River on the western side of the Park. They followed the Madison to the Firehole River before turning south to the Lower Geyser Basin, where they intended spending a couple of weeks fishing, hunting, camping, and exploring nearby areas, including the Basin with its variety of thermal features. One night they camped near Castle Geyser, "which by way of reception, gave a night eruption, covering us with spray and making a most unearthly noise," Emma Cowan later wrote. She and her party visited the area around the Yellowstone Falls, some in the group rode as far south as Yellowstone Lake, and during their visit they met General Sherman, who told them of the battle between the Nez Percés and the army at the Big Hole on August 9–10.

"The scout who was with the General's party assured us we would be perfectly safe if we would remain in the Basin, as the Indians would never come into the Park," Emma wrote, taking note that Sherman and his men were now departing. By August 23, the Cowans had gathered at their main camp in the Lower Geyser Basin and made plans for their own departure. They spent their last night in the place they called geyserland sitting around the campfire, singing and telling stories.

The Madison River Valley, indeed most of the Yellowstone country, offered the Nez Percés abundant game and ample grass for their hundreds of horses. As the main party moved slowly along the river, Yellow Wolf was scouting alone, as he often did, when several other Nez Percés joined him. These men rode up the Madison several miles ahead of Joseph and the main band of Indians, stopping at the confluence with the Gibbon River when they heard the sound of someone chopping a tree.

John Shively, a fifty-two-year-old prospector en route from

the Black Hills of South Dakota to Montana, had met with the Cowan party earlier in the day and made plans to travel to Radersburg with them the following morning. He was in his solitary camp on the evening of August 23, chopping wood for his supper fire, when he heard a noise, looked up, and found four Indians standing ten feet from his fire. "He was cooking," Yellow Wolf recalled the incident. "We got up to him, one on each side, in back of him. We grabbed him." The Nez Percés, unfamiliar with Yellowstone, thought Shively could guide them through the Park, so some of them took the prospector to the main Indian camp, then situated along the Madison.

Yellow Wolf and his companions continued their scouting until they spotted a campfire about a half mile from Shively's camp, but did not approach as night fell, since the ground was unstable from geyser activity.

The following morning, August 24, strange voices awoke Emma Cowan. When she peered from under her tent she saw Indians in the camp—Yellow Wolf and the other Nez Percé scouts. The tourists made efforts to communicate with the Indians, gave them a small amount of food, and then packed to leave as they had intended the night before. When everything had been stowed in the wagon and buggy, the Cowan party started toward home accompanied by the Indians. Eventually Yellow Wolf instructed the tourists to turn east, travel along a stream later called Nez Percé Creek, and follow a barely discernable trail through a pine forest to Mary Lake. Burned trees had fallen and blocked the path, forcing the tourists to abandon their carriage and wagon and continue on horseback while the Nez Percés looted the wagon, broke spokes from the wheels, and took the clothing and supplies. The Indians then took the Cowans' healthy, rested horses and gave them worn-out animals in exchange.

Although at the time the Cowan party had no idea of his presence, John Shively was also traveling with the Indians, riding farther ahead. Lean Elk, still responsible for the Nez Percé march, kept an eye on the captives and restrained younger warriors who still sought revenge for the attack on their families at the Big Hole. On the way up the trail toward Mary Lake, Lean Elk told the Cowans they could leave. Men in their party escaped into the woods while Emma and her family backtracked until younger warriors surrounded them, shot George Cowan in the leg and then in the head, and threatened the others. Lean Elk and a Nez Percé named Red Scout had followed the tourists to see to their safety, came upon the attack, and stopped the young warriors from further harming the tourists. With Red Scout's help, Lean Elk took Emma Cowan and her siblings, Frank and Ida Carpenter, back into custody, leaving George Cowan, who was presumed dead, beside the trail.

Most of the day Frank Carpenter rode with or near Lean Elk. That night both Frank and Emma were kept in Joseph's camp and there learned that Ida was with Looking Glass, in a location across a meadow from the makeshift shelters housing Joseph and his family. Frank Carpenter tried to talk with Joseph, but the chief, wearing a single eagle feather in his hair, paid him little attention as he sat "sombre and silent" by the fire. "Grave and dignified, he looked a chief," Emma recalled. When her brother picked up an Indian baby lying on a blanket and handed the child to Emma, Joseph's countenance changed and she saw the "glimmer of a smile on his face, showing that he had heart beneath the stony exterior." This baby may have been his youngest daughter, for the woman with Joseph was "all smiles, showing her white teeth," Emma said. Joseph's older daughter was present as well.

The Indian woman in Joseph's camp tried to console Emma after learning that George Cowan had been shot and left for dead on the trail. She handed Emma a cup of willow bark tea, a common Indian drink that had the added benefit of being a painkiller since the cooked willow bark had the same properties as aspirin. Emma refused to drink the bitter tea that evening and also refused bread. As they settled for the night, Joseph rolled into a blanket and slept with his feet toward the campfire. Emma Cowan and Frank Carpenter sat closely together, also near the fire. When it began to rain, the Indian woman wrapped a piece of canvas around the two.

Lean Elk remained in charge of daily travel as the Nez Percés proceeded through the Yellowstone country, circling among the campfires when morning came to organize the day's march. His powerful voice echoed as he commanded them. On the second day after taking the white captives, the Indians spread out along the trail in a line nearly three miles long as they wove through the trees and across open meadows. Each family group traveled as a unit, with older boys herding their hundreds of loose horses ahead of the women and children. The women led pack horses and mules loaded with supplies, stopping to unpack them or force them backward when they became lodged between trees. Joseph traveled with the families, helped with the pack horses, kept the line moving, and assisted when a horse or mule balked or needed packs rearranged.

The Indians and the captives continued across Yellowstone Park and into the open meadowland of the Hayden Valley, before following the Yellowstone River upstream to Mud Volcano. There the stench of sulphur, mixed with the burping, bubbling sounds of superheated boiling mud, stung their noses as they plunged their horses across the river. At Pelican Valley in the southeast part of the Park, the Indians halted for the day, building fires for each family camp while women fished for supper. The open meadows beside the river provided rich grass for their animals, lean and worn-out from being on the trail for nearly three months.

During the day Indian scouts brought word of more tourists camped near the Yellowstone Falls to the north. Some scouts watched the back trail for Howard and his troops while, in camp, the Indian women, assisted by Frank Carpenter, hauled water and baked bread. They again made willow bark tea and this night Emma Cowan drank some of it, but she refused to eat the fish, which she said had been "cut in two, dumped into an immense camp-kettle filled with water and boiled to a pulp. The formality of cleaning [the fish] had not entered into the formula."

During the evening Nez Percé warriors and headmen joined Joseph and Lean Elk in council near their fire. Emma and her siblings could not understand what was being said but knew at least a part of the discussion involved their fate, with Joseph arguing on their behalf. The following morning, Lean Elk took the captives, gave them two horses to ride, helped them cross the Yellowstone River, showed them a trail, and told them to "go quick." They made their way north steadily but cautiously until they met a military scouting party and provided information on the location of the Nez Percé camp, the Indians' direction of travel, and the condition of the people and their animals.

The day Emma Cowan and her siblings were released, Nez Percé scouts attacked the tourist party they had located near the Yellowstone Falls, killing one man and wounding another. They still had the miner John Shively along to serve as guide; he would spend eleven days with the Nez Percés, escaping only shortly before they left the Park and later remarking on how Joseph and Lean Elk had protected Emma and Ida.

By the time they reached Pelican Valley and released Emma and the Carpenters, the Nez Percés had been joined by a number of Shoshone Indians who knew that army troops supported by other Shoshones were prepared to stop the Nez Percés should they travel south into Wyoming. As they had intended from the onset, the Nez Percés and their families now turned toward the Crows' lands, following Pelican Valley, a broad, ten-mile-long area with abundant grass for the animals and plenty of elk, deer, and fish for the people. While in Yellowstone, the Indians traveled shorter distances each day, resting and recovering from what had already been a grueling trip. They separated into two major groups, one led by Joseph, the other commanded by Looking Glass, as they followed different drainages to Mist Creek Pass and then all descended to the Lamar River on the eastern side of the Park. This river country resembled their homeland, with steep canyon walls, open meadows for animal grazing, and a swift current where there were abundant fish for cooking pots. Again the group divided, allowing the Nez Percés to travel more slowly and still have plenty of feed for their horses.

Joseph led his people north along the Lamar, abandoning dozens of horses and mules that had been cut and injured as they negotiated the rugged terrain. Eventually Joseph also turned east, traveling out of Yellowstone. Indian scouts, meanwhile, continued to explore other portions of the Park; some went to Mammoth Hot Springs, where they raided a log cabin hotel, encountered tourists they'd already confronted at the Yellowstone Falls, and burned a bridge across the Yellowstone River. The scouts then backtracked along the Lamar River and rejoined Joseph.

The Nez Percé scouts had determined that soldiers blocked escape along the Yellowstone River into Montana and also contacted the Crow Indians in Montana's buffalo country. But instead of supporting the Nez Percés, as Looking Glass had promised during the council many weeks before at Weippe Prairie, the scouts learned that the Crows would not welcome the Nez Percés, would not take their side in the dispute, and, even more disturbing, had already scouted for the army force chasing Joseph and his people.

General Howard followed the Madison River into Yellowstone Park days after Joseph and the Nez Percés wove their way there and captured the first group of tourists. A party of Bannock Indians from southern Idaho, longtime enemies of the Nez Percés, had joined Howard's command just after the Camas Meadows raid and fight, and preceded the general into Yellowstone. Guided by Howard's chief of scouts, S. G. Fisher, the forty Bannocks trailed Joseph's people across the Park. The trail made by hundreds of horses was easy to follow, but once along the Lamar River, where the Nez Percés had split into smaller groups, it became difficult to determine where each band would depart Yellowstone. Along the way the Bannocks abandoned the pursuit and returned to their homes.

Howard's command, with its wagons for support, moved slower than Joseph and the Nez Percés or the general's own scouts. As when crossing Lolo Pass, Captain William F. Spurgin of the Twenty-first Infantry and his fifty-two civilian Skillets built a wagon road for the supply caravan. They cut trees that had fallen across the trail, moved rocks, and wielded picks and shovels to smooth the grade. On steep side hills, they attached ropes to the wagons, holding them steady to prevent them from overturning. In one precipitous descent to the Yellowstone River, which became known as Spurgin's Beaver Slide, they tied ropes to the back axles, wrapped them around sturdy trees, and cautiously lowered the wagons while the drivers stood in the nearly perpendicular wagon boxes and held the teams. Howard's party found George Cowan, not dead but seriously injured, and placed him in one of the wagons.

On September 4, Howard's force reached Mud Volcano and the Yellowstone River ford the Nez Percés had used and he ordered the men to bathe and wash clothing in the hot mineral springs. The wagons had stopped after their difficult descent to the Yellowstone River, and the following day Howard discharged the teamsters, telling them to make their way out of the Park. The soldiers now used pack mules to carry supplies. Howard himself abandoned the trail of the Nez Percés at the ford near Mud Volcano, following the Yellowstone downstream to the remains of the burned bridge and then riding east intending to close in on the Indians and corner them. He knew from messages received while he was in Yellowstone that Lieutenant Colonel Samuel D. Sturgis, with 450 mounted men of the Seventh Cavalry and several Crow Indian scouts, had moved into the Shoshone River country just east of Yellowstone. This force was poised to encounter Joseph and the Nez Percés as they left the Park but before they could cross onto the open plains of Montana's buffalo country. Sturgis, a Pennsylvanian, was an experienced Indian fighter, having engaged Jicarilla Apaches in the 1850s and Kiowas and Comanches on the Southern Plains in the '60s.

Joseph and the other headmen recombined their parties in the Sunlight Basin, a big hole ringed by mountains just east of Yellowstone. To move out of it they could cross over the steep mountains forming part of the Absaroka Range or they could venture near the narrow defile of the Clark's Fork River. This canyon was as rugged and seemingly impenetrable as those in the upper reaches of the Snake River near Joseph's Wallowa homeland. To the dismay of Sturgis and Howard, the headmen chose the river route and on September 8 again gave the army the slip.

The Nez Percés exited Clark's Fork and headed north, back into Montana, with Lean Elk still in charge of the daily travel. The Crows would not help them and since they could not remain in the buffalo country along the Yellowstone River as intended, they revised their plans. They would travel another three hundred or more miles to Canada and join Sitting Bull, the Hunkpapa leader who had escaped there after the June 1876 battle at the Little Bighorn. The Nez Percés had few past dealings with the Lakotas and once had sided with the Crows in a battle against them, but now they would take their chances that Sitting Bull and his people, in exile north of the Canadian border, would support and welcome them.

The thirteen days the Nez Percés spent in crossing through Yellowstone, while giving them a chance to rest and recuperate, allowed the military ample opportunity to get into position. Sturgis, though thwarted in his first effort to stop them as they departed the Park, remained in striking distance and Howard still pushed from behind. There were now hundreds of troops surrounding the Indians, closing in to check their flight.

We Could Have Escaped

What started as an obscure army-versus-Indian campaign in a remote mountain valley in Idaho became a national drama as the Nez Percés crossed Idaho, Montana, Yellowstone National Park, and northwestern Wyoming. At first, regional newspaper correspondents such as Thomas Sutherland of the Portland *Daily Standard* and writers for the Owyhee *Avalanche* and Lewiston *Teller* in Idaho kept the public apprised of the events, but the capture of tourists at Yellowstone brought increased newspaper attention to Joseph and his people. By the time the Nez Percés emerged from the Park the story of their hegira was headlined all across America.

Because Joseph had such a prominent role in negotiations prior to the outbreak of hostilities and since removal of his band from the Wallowa Valley of Oregon to the reservation in Idaho had been the pivotal decision by federal authorities, the newspapers attributed virtually all the Nez Percés kills, tactics, and strategies to him. Since there were no reporters traveling with Joseph and the Nez Percés, his councils with headmen and warriors—where all important decisions were reached—went unrecorded. Readers of the day became familiar only with "Joseph's War"; he was lionized as the great war chief of the Nez Percés, and the successes and failures of the war were all attributed to him.

Frontier army commanders and troops likewise credited Joseph with full leadership of the Indians, particularly when it came to their military-like actions and when the Nez Percés bested the army, as had occurred early in the war at White Bird Canyon, Fort Fizzle, Camas Meadows, and now the passage through Yellowstone. The success of Joseph's people in these engagements, and the embarrassing fact that a few hundred Indians and their families, with a couple of thousand head of horses, had eluded an ever-growing army force, began to draw not only attention but also empathy from people following the story and, in some cases, from the very troops who pursued the Nez Percés. "I am actually beginning to admire their bravery and endurance in the face of so many well equipped enemies," Howard's field surgeon, Dr. John Fitz-Gerald, said.

Such was not the view, however, of the army's supreme commander, General William T. Sherman, who barely missed running headlong into the Indians during his tour of Yellowstone Park in August. He suggested harsh action: "Their horses, arms and property should be taken away. Many of their leaders [should be] executed," he said, and offered the view that other tribal members "should be treated like the Modocs, sent to some other country; there should be extreme severity."

Sherman, like other military commanders, believed that most of the tribesmen "will fight hard, skillfully, to the death."

East of Yellowstone, the Nez Percés pushed through the Clark's Fork River Canyon, surprising military strategists who did not think the route feasible for the hundreds of Indians with their great horse herd. Joseph maintained his role as protector of the People, directing and assisting the families as they made their way, day by day, toward freedom. They were riding through Crow country when warriors scouting ahead came upon the stagecoach serving the region as it stopped at a ranch along the Yellowstone River. The men swooped down, frightened away the three passengers, tossed aside the mail, burned the ranch, tied their own horses to the back of the coach, and went for a ride, whipping the horses pulling it into a fast gallop across the prairie. Their frivolity ended quickly when they spied army scouts watching them. They abandoned the coach and joined the others then being pursued by troops from the Sixth and Seventh Cavalry commanded by Lieutenant Colonel Samuel Sturgis.

The Indian families had nearly reached Canyon Creek, just north of the Yellowstone River, when troops broke over the horizon. The Indians picked up their pace and disappeared into the chasm through which the creek meandered, as warriors positioned themselves on high ridges above the entrance to the defile, protecting the rear and halting the military advance.

A brief skirmish with the troops followed during which

the Nez Percés killed two enlisted men with the Seventh Cavalry and wounded another dozen troopers. One Indian died in the fighting and three more were wounded, but more significant, the Crow scouts who rode with the soldiers and who had fast, fresh animals for the pursuit captured dozens of the Nez Percés' extra ponies.

The military's failure to stop the Nez Percés as they exited Yellowstone, and the skirmish at Canyon Creek that delayed but did not stop their forward movement, resulted in yet another military force being launched against them.

General O. O. Howard, plagued by weary men and horses and suffering from limited supplies after following the Indians across rough lands impossible for wagons, asked Colonel Nelson A. Miles, commander at the Cantonment on Tongue River in eastern Montana, to "make every effort in your power to prevent the escape of this hostile band, and at least to hold them in check until I can overtake them."

A thirty-eight-year-old career soldier from Massachusetts, Miles was at this point in his career aiming to upgrade his rank to brigadier general.* He took to the field against the Nez Percés on September 18, just over three months since their flight began. However, as commander at the Cantonment, later called Fort Keogh, he already had been orchestrating troop movement to support Howard.

Miles was an experienced Indian fighter, a field commander during action on the Southern Plains against Comanches, Kiowas, and Southern Cheyennes, three years

---

*In 1892 he received the Medal of Honor for his actions with the Army of the Potomac at Chancellorsville during the Civil War.

earlier. More significant, he was intimately familiar with the country the Nez Percés were then crossing. In 1876–77 he had been involved in the winter campaign to force free-ranging Lakotas and Northern Cheyenne Indians onto reservations. Those efforts resulted in the eventual surrender of the Lakota war chief Crazy Horse and the Northern Cheyennes under the leadership of Dull Knife. Miles had pursued Sitting Bull into Canada during the recent winter campaign and still monitored the Hunkpapa medicine man's band. In August, Miles warned Colonel Sturgis and General Howard that Sitting Bull may have moved back into the United States and even then might be on his way toward the Missouri River to eventually join with the Nez Percés.

The military needed to strike a "decisive blow" against the Nez Percés, "bringing them into complete subjection to the Government," Miles wrote Sturgis in August as he told of Sitting Bull's movement, urging Sturgis to stay between the Lakota band and the Nez Percés. Later Miles sent messages to his fellow officer recommending a surrender strategy for the Nez Percés but immediately followed with a contradictory message: "I would prefer that you strike the Nez Percés a severe blow if possible before sending any word to surrender."

Orders from Howard had then drawn Sturgis toward Sunlight Basin in Wyoming where the Nez Percés outmaneuvered him, and they now rode toward Sitting Bull. Howard knew his weary men could not overtake the Nez Percés, but he thought possibly Miles could catch them.

Miles left his post on the Yellowstone on September 18 commanding 520 men from multiple units of his own Fifth Infantry plus troops from the Second and Seventh Cavalry, including Cheyenne Indian scouts and civilian employees. They intended to intercept the Nez Percés before they reached the Missouri River, if possible, and certainly before they could get across the boundary into Canada to join the Lakotas.

When General Howard learned Miles was in the field and poised to cut off the Nez Percés, he slowed his advance. He had found that each time he had backed off pursuit, the Indians also reduced their pace; they had done so in crossing the Lolo Trail and through Montana's Bitterroot Valley while he held up at the Clearwater River in Idaho. They had reduced their rate of travel as they moved through Yellowstone while he resupplied following the raid at Camas Meadows. Now he hoped they would slow their march again, giving Miles the opportunity to sweep ahead of them.

The strain of constant movement began eroding Nez Percé solidarity following the skirmish at Canyon Creek. The people were tired, and their horses were exhausted, weak, and becoming lame. Lean Elk's rigid schedule became wearing, and the headmen argued more as they saw the families struggling from one campsite to the next. Elderly and injured Indians were left behind; women dropped out of the line to bear children alone and then catch up to their families as best they could, some never returning to the perilous trail. The tension was strongest between Lean Elk and Looking Glass. White Bird and Toolhoolhoolzote maintained quiet composure, and Joseph's influence increased. He had already proven that he could command the hundreds of family members and keep them successfully moving toward freedom; after Canyon

Creek he became more assertive with the warriors and other headmen. Always respected by the people, he now began assuming the mantle of full authority for them. It was a role that would become vital in a few short weeks.

Their course was clearly set now. The Indians would trail almost due north across the open plains and rolling country, prime buffalo habitat. Howard had slowed his advance, and the Indians knew it and once again believed they might be able to outrun the army to find sanctuary and safety in Canada with Sitting Bull.

Day after weary day, the Nez Percés traveled through Montana, crossing open plains and badlands, skirting mountains, fording streams or finding only alkali water. The trail swung through the Judith Gap, where Colonel Miles had anticipated they might try to hide, and they then headed toward the Missouri River, arriving at a ford near Cow Island on September 23.

The Missouri served as a main conduit for freight and supplies needed in Montana Territory by both civilians and military commands and had been plied routinely by steamboats since the gold boom of 1863–64. In the early months of the year steamboats could navigate the river as far upstream as Fort Benton, but late in the season, with river flows reduced, bigger boats could only travel to the landing at Cow Island, around eighty miles downstream from Benton. In 1877, a dozen civilian engineers were at Cow Island making improvements to the river channel to facilitate future steamboat travel and ten soldiers from the Seventh Cavalry were at the site to guard tons of freight held there. Since there were no permanent buildings at their temporary post, the men lived in tents and had dug a drainage ditch around their encampment and built an embankment that provided limited protection from an Indian attack.

When the Nez Percés reached the Cow Island ford, a party of warriors crossed the Missouri first to provide defense for their families should the soldiers make any offensive move. Once north of the Missouri the Nez Percé families traveled another couple of miles, halted for the day, and made camp. The few troops and civilians at the freight landing had not become aggressive, so Joseph and Looking Glass, with dozens of men supporting them, rode back and requested supplies from the fifty tons of military and commercial freight stacked there awaiting transportation upriver to Fort Benton. The Nez Percés met Sergeant William Moelchert of the Seventh Cavalry and asked for food from among the stores at the landing. He refused and they offered to pay. He again refused. "They came back a third time and pleaded with me for something to eat," Moelchert said.

"I went back to the breastworks and put a side of bacon in a sack filled about half full with hardtack, took it out to them and they very kindly thanked me for the same."

A side of bacon and half a sack of hardtack was a pitiful offering to seven hundred hungry people camped within easy striking distance of the military position and its tons of freight. During the night the Indians attacked, not with the intention of killing the soldiers and civilians at the post but to feed their people. They took flour, sugar, coffee, bacon, and beans, plus pots and pans, and burned many of the remaining stores, so that the supplies could not be used by the army pursuing them. In the raids, the Nez Percés killed one soldier approaching the landing and injured two civilians. Defenders wounded one Indian. Clearly, the nearly two hundred warriors in the attack could have overwhelmed the dozen or so defenders at Cow Landing had that been their intent.

The following night Joseph's people halted a couple of miles from a wagon train and cattle herd owned by O. G. Cooper. Some members of the tribe talked with Cooper and freighters in the train, seeking to purchase ammunition from them. "The young sprightly bucks had but a few cartridges in their belts, while the old fellows, and the middle-aged, seemed better supplied," Cooper said later. "I think they were all short of ammunition, as they were very anxious to buy them from us." The Indians carried a variety of guns, including cavalry carbines. "Their animals were very poor, and many had sore backs and feet," Cooper said.

The next morning as Cooper began rounding up his cattle, the Nez Percés attacked and plundered the wagon train, killing three of the teamsters. That same day, September 25, additional troops from Fort Benton reached Cow Island after the Indian raid there, followed the Nez Percés, and engaged the Indians at Cow Creek Canyon, where one citizen volunteer was killed. The Indians left behind twenty wounded, crippled, or dead horses.

As they continued their journey north after these skirmishes, the tension between the headmen flared again. The people were now just eighty miles from the Canadian border and Looking Glass again assumed primary leadership for them, replacing Lean Elk. Almost immediately the travel pace slowed. The Nez Percés knew that Colonel Sturgis and General Howard were at least a couple of days in the rear; they had just bested the few troops sent from Fort Benton and had no idea of any other soldiers in the field.

Under Looking Glass they put another forty miles behind

them and, despite disagreement among the headmen, complied with his order to make camp on Snake Creek at noon on September 29. They had only another forty miles to travel before they reached Canada. That day the men hunted buffalo to replenish supplies and during the afternoon women began preserving the hides. Their camp was at the edge of the Bear's Paw Mountains in a rolling hill country with rugged bluffs to the south and a ridge on the east. Snake Creek ran beside their makeshift shelters and there was plenty of late-season grass on a plateau to the west for their horses. There was no wood for fires, so dried buffalo dung was used and the area called Tsanim Alikos Pah, "Place of the Manure Fire."

Colonel Miles and his five hundred troops began their forced march across eastern Montana on September 18, leaving the Yellowstone River and traveling northwest. They learned that the Nez Percés had crossed the Musselshell River, so continued at a rapid pace toward the Missouri, also crossing that river after the Indians had done so. Troops with Miles saw deer, buffalo, and antelope all across the country they traversed on September 29, and they could see the Bear's Paw Mountains toward their southwest. It began raining that afternoon and, as the temperature dropped, flakes of snow fell. Late in the day a courier reached Miles with a message from General Howard, who said he would halt his pursuit of the Nez Percés and send his own cavalry home. Howard's infantry and the men commanded by Colonel Sturgis would remain at the Missouri River for a few days longer. This message, Miles knew, meant he could expect no immediate support should he encounter the Nez Percés.

Meantime, in the Indian camp, men who had been out hunting reported seeing people moving across the prairie, perhaps one of the Indian bands who inhabited the area. Although the other headmen and some warriors recommended sending out scouts, Looking Glass did not do so.

Miles, however, did have scouts ranging far from his main column, and they returned to him late on September 29 to say they had located the Nez Percé trail and knew the camp was nearby.

Joseph and his daughter Sound of Running Water were at the horse herd early on the morning of September 30, preparing to break camp, when they heard the cry "Soldiers, soldiers, soldiers!" as Cheyenne Indian scouts and Seventh Cavalry troopers broke over the ridge and swept toward the Nez Percé camp. "We had no knowledge of General Miles's army until a short time before he charged upon us, cutting our camp in two and capturing nearly all of our horses," Joseph said. "My little daughter, twelve years of age, was with me. I gave her a rope and told her to catch a horse and join those who were separated from the camp."

The cold morning erupted into chaos as the Indians frantically tried to catch horses, mount them, and race away from the soldiers. In the camp some of the warriors began shooting in defense. "I thought of my wife and my other children, now surrounded by soldiers," Joseph said, "and I resolved to go to them or die."

Swinging aboard his horse, "with a prayer to the Great Spirit Chief, I dashed unarmed through the line of soldiers. My clothes were cut to pieces and my horse was wounded, but

I was not hurt." In the camp with soldiers all around, Joseph rode to his own makeshift lodge and there, he said, "My wife handed me my rifle, saying, 'Here's your gun. Fight!'"

That morning Colonel Nelson Miles had on sky blue trousers, a red shirt, a short buckskin coat, and black boots. He wore a broad-brimmed slouch hat with a blue ribbon around the crown that trailed down his back, and even had on a black necktie. When his scouts returned with specific details about the Nez Percé camp, the two-hundred-pound colonel, his brown mustache and full sideburns neatly trimmed, began snapping orders. He placed the Seventh Cavalry in the lead of his formation, with the Second Cavalry and Fifth Infantry soldiers who were mounted to follow in succession. The foot soldiers of the Fifth Infantry would trail their mounted counterparts. Each man carried one hundred rounds of ammunition and most wore wool greatcoats against the chill of the season. Miles sent a message for artillery and a wagon train that supported the troops to proceed forward as rapidly as possible.

Earlier in the morning Nez Percé riders who had been north of their own camp saw buffalo running across the plains and warned Looking Glass that soldiers must be nearby. This message reinforced a dream by Wottolen that they would be attacked, yet Looking Glass made no move for a hasty departure. Nez Percés riding out from their camp spotted the army bearing down on them just as Miles gave the final order to advance. The Nez Percés raced back to spread the alarm.

The Cheyennes who scouted for Miles first encountered

the Nez Percé outriders, and when they fled toward their own people the Cheyennes returned to Miles's position. There they stripped to breechclouts, painted themselves for war, donned feathered headdresses, caught fresh war horses, and then raced off toward Joseph's camp.

The Nez Percé children were playing that morning in camp using sticks to throw mud balls. "I looked up and saw a spotted horse, a Cheyenne warrior, wearing a war bonnet," White Bird's son said. "He was closely followed by the troops. . . . Bullets were flying." The children ran, most of them barefoot. They crossed the creek and fled toward the horses. "I had only a shirt as clothing," the boy said. "Cold, wet, I was freezing . . . one woman showed pity for me. She took me up behind her."

Nez Percé women and children who reached the herd caught horses, made makeshift bridles, some from pieces of blanket, and fled north toward Canada. Warriors who had found their horses counter-attacked the soldiers as they defended first one portion of their camp, then another. "We rode the lead-cut air," Shot in Head said. "Bullets were buzzing like summer flies."

Miles's troopers attacked with a vengeance. Yellow Wolf watched "hundreds of soldiers charging in two wide, circling wings. They were surrounding our camp."

"I called my men to drive them back. We fought at close range, not more than twenty steps apart," Joseph said. Some soldiers fell in the Indian camp and the Nez Percés took their guns and ammunition as they repulsed three separate onslaughts by the troopers.

Bullets flew in every direction, felling soldiers and Indians alike, including Lean Elk, who was mistakenly downed by a

Nez Percé gunshot, and Ollokot, hit in the head by a soldier's bullet as he crouched behind a rock and fired at the enemy.

"The soldiers kept up a continuous fire," Joseph said. "Six of my men were killed in one spot near me."

Nez Percé fighters, who could not return to the surrounded camp, fought from gullies and ravines during the day and crept through enemy lines that night to rejoin their families.

The day ended in misery for both sides.

Dozens of Miles's troops had been killed or wounded. Dead soldiers lay within the Indian camp, and wounded men close to the Indians could not be rescued, since Nez Percé sharpshooters hit or killed those who entered the range of their carbines. For the same reason, Indian dead and wounded, including the body of Toolhoolhoolzote, lay on the open battlefield.

The Nez Percé women used their camas digging sticks and butcher knives to excavate shelter pits and to burrow tunnels between these fortifications. The women and children slept in the shelters; the warriors were protected in their rifle pits. They had no fires. Children cried from the cold. Many Nez Percés had been wounded and twenty-two killed, including leaders Ollokot, Lean Elk, and Toolhoolhoolzote. The Nez Percé death wail cut through the night.

To add to the turmoil, rain fell that evening and by morning snow blanketed the Bear's Paw battleground. Neither Indians nor soldiers could find adequate buffalo chips for fires, or they feared starting a fire that would reveal their location, and all suffered, huddled in their makeshift shelters against the wet and cold night.

In their camp, the Nez Percés faced tough decisions. "We could have escaped from Bear Paw Mountain if we had left our wounded, old women, and children behind," Joseph said. "We were unwilling to do this."

The battle of the Bear's Paw became a siege when Miles realized the Indians had entrenched. Although he could launch additional attacks, to do so would lead to heavy casualties among his men. "I have this day surprised the hostile Nez Percés in their camp and have had a very sharp fight," he wrote in a message to General Howard sent late September 30. "Please move forward with caution and rapidity."

I Will Fight No More

A single line of dark forms marched across the open prairie as early-morning mist and wind swept over the soldiers at the Bear's Paw battleground on October 1, 1877. Colonel Nelson Miles watched the shapes, fearing Sitting Bull and the Lakotas had learned of the previous day's battle from Nez Percés who escaped on horseback and fled north. To Miles's relief, the orderly line turned out to be a herd of buffalo advancing before a storm.

During the previous night, soldiers had positioned a Hotchkiss breech-loading mountain gun at the south end of the Indian camp. This prototype military weapon could launch a two-pound percussion shell nearly a mile, and the current battle marked its debut use in the field. The gun and carriage weighed just over 300 pounds, could be hauled by only one or two mules, and was loaded and fired by a crew of two. Under cover of darkness, infantrymen, with weapons accurate at longer distances than cavalry carbines, moved forward as the cavalry troopers withdrew, and field surgeons set up a hospital tent.

In the Nez Percé camp, Joseph, White Bird, and Looking Glass knew that some people had escaped the day's fighting and were even then headed toward Canada to find Sitting Bull and urge him to come to their aid. In their dugouts the Indians had food remaining from stores they'd plundered at Cow Island and could carve meat from dead horses. The Nez Percés had water in nearby Snake Creek, but since they could reach that source only when darkness hid their movements, they excavated two water holes and collected water using buffalo horn dippers. They believed they could hold out until Sitting Bull came.

Sitting Bull's Lakota band eluded frontier soldiers after the Little Bighorn battle of June 1876 by fleeing north and crossing into Canada, where United States troops could not pursue them. Their camp was about eighty miles north of the Bear's Paw battlefield, but it took several days for the Nez Percés who escaped the attack of September 30 to close that distance and find the Lakotas. Even then, Sitting Bull did not immediately head south to aid the Nez Percés. The two tribes could not easily communicate, and he believed Joseph's people were farther from his camp than they actually were. Moreover, Canadian officials at Saskatchewan, near Sitting Bull's camp, discouraged him from giving aid. They told the Lakota that if he and his warriors crossed the border—the Medicine Line—

they would not be allowed to return to Canada. So, while Joseph, White Bird, and Looking Glass watched for Sitting Bull's arrival, he remained in his own camp.

Throughout the first day of fighting, Miles in his red shirt, sky blue pants, and buckskin coat had ridden around the battlefield and called upon the Indians to surrender. Now the headmen discussed that option. White Bird said the Nez Percés should escape and continue their flight to Canada. Looking Glass argued for patience until Sitting Bull arrived. Only Joseph counseled surrender as he heard the pitiful cries of the children and the stoic silence of the old people, many of them injured during past battles. On October 1 when Miles dispatched a messenger with a white flag, Joseph sent his trusted tribesman Yellow Bull to meet him.

"Yellow Bull understood the messenger to say that Colonel Miles wished me to consider the situation, that he did not want to kill my people unnecessarily," Joseph said, although his friend questioned whether the colonel was in earnest. "I sent him back with my answer, that I had not made up my mind but would think about it and send word soon."

Later, three Cheyenne scouts rode near the Nez Percé fortifications, communicated with the besieged people, and saw dead Indians lying in the camp. These men informed Joseph that they believed Miles sincerely wanted peace. Both sides cautiously agreed to a truce under which they allowed wounded and dead to be retrieved. Then Joseph walked to Miles's tent.

"Come, let us sit by the fire and talk this matter over," Miles told Joseph.

The Nez Percé told the colonel he wanted to ease the suffering of the young children and older people in his camp, but he and his followers could not relinquish all of their guns as demanded by Miles because without them they could not hunt for food. Further, Looking Glass, White Bird, and other Indians would not surrender. Unable to resolve differences, Joseph left Miles in his tent and began to walk back to his own camp. As Joseph departed the military enclave, Miles ordered soldiers to detain him. This violated the truce that had led Joseph to enter the soldier camp and further infuriated his people behind their own fortifications.

Lieutenant Lovell H. Jerome, Company H, Second Cavalry, a thirty-eight-year-old New Yorker and West Pointer, thwarted whatever plans Miles had envisioned when he detained Joseph. That same day Jerome and some Cheyenne scouts crept near the Indian camp to discover how the Nez Percés had arranged their rifle pits and whether soldiers could launch a successful assault. The tribesmen observed this surveillance and when they learned Miles had taken Joseph prisoner they captured the lieutenant. Some in the Indian camp wanted to kill Jerome immediately, but Yellow Bull and Wottolen protected the soldier throughout the night. They placed him in one of the dugout shelters, provided him with food sent from the army's supplies, allowed him to send a message to Miles, and, astonishingly, even let him retain his pistol. By comparison, Joseph spent the night in the mule pen, bound up in a blanket.

Jerome's capture incensed the soldiers with Miles who knew the colonel had intended to take Joseph, withdraw from the battlefield, and entrench. Now Miles could not proceed without risking Jerome's life. "The fact is he was very anxious, as all of us were, lest Sitting Bull should come to the Nez Percés' assistance," Jerome said. "I can attest that the Nez Percés really expected that Sitting Bull would aid them." Joseph himself said, "I knew that we were near Sitting Bull's camp in King George's land [Canada], and I thought maybe the Nez Percés who had escaped would return with assistance."

During that night the fighting resumed, and on the morning of October 2 Yellow Bull was permitted to enter the American command area to determine Joseph's condition, although Colonel Miles refused to allow the two to talk privately. Later in the day, with hostages on each side, Miles agreed that Joseph could return to his camp, following which Jerome was released. "With the suspicion of treachery on both sides, thirteen of our men lay in their trenches scarcely forty rods off, with the rifles held at a dead rest on Joseph and my three Indian guides," Jerome said. "More than twenty Indians had an equally sure sight over their Winchesters and Henrys straight at Colonel Miles and me."

Now Joseph met with White Bird and Looking Glass. Although they had voiced differing opinions many times during the past four months, the leaders had always held together in the end. They agreed that each had the right to choose his own path and that even their individual followers could decide their own course. White Bird remained adamant against surrender. Looking Glass told Joseph he knew about "a man of two faces and two tongues. If you surrender you will be sorry."

"The white captain has made good talk all right," Joseph said. "Many of our people are out in the hills, naked and freezing. The women are suffering with cold, the children crying with the chilly dampness of the shelter pits. For myself I do not care. It is for them I am going to surrender."

Looking Glass remonstrated with Joseph and declared he would never surrender. He then smoked his pipe and talked with the warriors until someone called out that there was an Indian approaching the camp. When Looking Glass stood for a better view, believing the Indian might be Sitting Bull, a bullet fired by one of Miles's men struck him in the head.

Looking Glass became the last Nez Percé fighter to die at the Bear's Paw battleground.

The impasse continued for another three days as Miles's force periodically attacked the entrenched Indians, although with little effect even with the aid of the Hotchkiss gun and other artillery. Everyone suffered from the cold, snowy, windy weather. On the evening of October 4, General O. O. Howard reached the battlefield along with interpreter Ad Chapman, the man who fired the first shot against the Indians at White Bird Canyon back in June. Despite that fact, the Nez Percés knew Chapman and trusted him.

"We could now talk understandingly," Joseph said. "Miles said to me in plain words, 'If you will come out and give up your arms, I will spare your lives and send you back to the reservation.'"

Two Nez Percé scouts, Old George and Captain John, arrived at the battlefield with Howard. Each of these old men, who had daughters in Joseph's camp, entered the Indian enclave to talk with him. The nontreaty Indians knew Commanding General William T. Sherman had earlier said their leaders and top fighters should be executed upon surrender, as had happened with the Modocs, but now Old George and Captain John assured them all their lives would be spared if they would quit the fight.

Now only Joseph and White Bird remained to lead the Nez Percés. Having tried for years to avoid war, and after enduring four months of constant movement that had debilitated his people, Joseph said, "I could not bear to see my wounded men and women suffer any longer; we had lost enough already. My people needed rest. We wanted peace."

In the shelter pits, with his weary, wounded people around him, Joseph made his decision. To Old George and Captain John he said, "Tell General Howard I know his heart. I am tired of fighting. Our chiefs are killed. Looking Glass is dead. Toolhoolhoolzote is dead. The old men are all dead. He who led on the young men is dead." This statement must have been especially difficult for Joseph, because the leader of the young men had been his younger brother Ollokot, whom he had trusted beyond all other men and who had often spoken on his behalf.

Joseph continued, "The little children are freezing to death. My people, some of them, have run away to the hills, and have no blankets, no food; no one knows where they are—perhaps freezing to death. I want to have time to look for my children and see how many of them I can find. Maybe I shall find them among the dead. Hear me, my chiefs. I am tired; my heart is sick and sad. From where the sun now stands I will fight no more forever."

Joseph's surrender speech became the defining statement of his life and of his people. It was relayed to Howard by the two scouts and recorded by the general's aide-de-camp, Charles Erskine Scott Wood. After the scouts delivered his message, Joseph mounted a horse that had been concealed in the camp to prevent its being shot during the five days of fighting. He slumped in his saddle, held his Winchester carbine across the pommel, and clasped a grey blanket around his shoulders. His face stoic, his long hair hanging in two braids over his chest and pompadour tied up with a piece of otter fur, he wore buckskin moccasins, leggings, and a war shirt, the latter ripped and torn by bullets. He had welts on his wrists and forehead where bullets had grazed his body. Joseph's most loyal warriors walked beside him as he approached the army's commanders and extended the Winchester to Colonel Miles.

Miles, according to Joseph, "had promised that we might return to our country with what stock we had left. I thought we could start again. I believed [him], or I never would have surrendered."

Once Joseph surrendered, the warriors in his band, singly and in pairs, came into the soldier camp and turned over their own weapons. The women and children then walked from their shelter pits toward fires in Miles's camp where they ate their first hot meal in five days.

Among the sixty-seven warriors who surrendered with Joseph on October 5, 1877, were members of the Palouse band led by Naked Head, a man who had pledged fealty to Joseph when he joined the Nez Percés on the Camas Prairie of Idaho in June.

During the night, the army remained vigilant, since many of the Nez Percés had not surrendered with Joseph. When it was fully dark, White Bird led close to fifty people from the shelter pits and with them slipped through the army lines to walk toward Canada. The following morning, when General Howard learned that White Bird had fled, he announced that the surrender conditions agreed to by Joseph were no longer valid. But as Joseph had earlier argued, he spoke and took action only for himself and the people who chose to follow him. His surrender did not extend to White Bird or anyone else who chose not to support it.

People from the Toolhoolhoolzote and Looking Glass bands followed Joseph in surrender, including two of Looking Glass's wives, whom Joseph later took as his own. However, as was their right under Nez Percé custom, some from Joseph's group, including Wetatonmi, Ollokot's surviving wife, did not follow him to the army camp but instead sought sanctuary in Canada with White Bird and Sitting Bull. Joseph's own wife Bear Crossing and daughter Sound of Running Water fled to Canada among the first wave of people to escape the Bear's Paw battle. His daughter never again lived with her father.

Of the seven hundred souls who had camped along Snake Creek near the Bear's Paw Mountains at noon on September 29, 1877, Miles eventually held 448 as prisoners of war. Twenty-five had died on the battlefield and the remainder had made their way toward Canada.

Somebody Has Our Horses

On October 7, soldiers and Nez Percés began the
265-mile march from the Bear's Paw battlefield to
the Cantonment on Tongue River in southeastern
Montana where the Tongue and Yellowstone rivers merged.
The troops had fashioned travois for the injured Indians and
placed wounded soldiers in wagons on beds of willow
branches and grass. The Nez Percés mounted their own recovered horses, and the soldiers encircled them as Colonel Nelson Miles set a smart pace, knowing winter would soon lock
the country in an icy grip.

Two weeks later, when word reached the Cantonment that
Miles's force and the Indians would soon ferry across the Yellowstone to the post, nearly everyone there rushed out to greet
them. The Fifth Infantry band lined up beneath a huge lone
cottonwood tree on the south bank of the river to play "Hail
to the Chief" as the post cannon boomed. Women, wearing
long riding skirts and broad-brimmed hats, sat on their horses
craning their necks to find their husbands while children and

dogs scurried around yelling and barking in the excitement. The troops who had remained at the post hustled a twelve-pound Napoléon gun and a three-inch ordnance rifle to the riverbank as a show of force and stood scrutinizing the ferry as it transported the military men and their Indian captives across the water. There to document the event was twenty-eight-year-old Ohioan John Fouch, who came west in 1876 and made the first post-battle photographs of the Little Bighorn battlefield. Now he was at the Cantonment as the post's official photographer.

When the Nez Percés reached the Yellowstone on October 23, Fouch set up his cumbersome equipment and captured stereoscopic images as the ferryboat disgorged its passengers. During the next week he took a photograph of Joseph dressed in a beaded buckskin shirt decorated with ermine tails and horsehair fringes, two blankets swaddling his legs, his braids wrapped in otter fur, a shell bracelet on his wrist, and three rings on his large scratched hands, two on his left and one on the right.

Before he departed by steamer down the Missouri River after the battle at the Bear's Paw, General Howard instructed Miles to care for the Nez Percés through the winter and to send them back to Idaho the following spring. "You will treat them as prisoners of war," Howard said, adding that his order stood "unless you receive instructions from higher authority."

Then, at Tongue River, with canvas issued to the Indians for shelters and Joseph's people making winter preparations, Miles heard from "higher authority": the Nez Percés "should never again be allowed to return to Oregon or to Lapwai,"

Commanding General Sherman said as he ordered the captives sent downriver to a post in North Dakota.

Miles opposed the decision, reporting to his superiors that five Nez Percés had died on the journey from Bear's Paw to the Cantonment and "others cannot live. I consider it inhuman to compel them to travel farther at this season of the year." But, his protests falling on deaf ears, he organized the healthiest Indians into one party to ride overland and arranged for a flotilla of flatboats to transport the others.

"You must not blame me," Miles told Joseph. "I have endeavored to keep my word, but the chief who is over me has given the order, and I must obey or resign. That would do you no good. Some other officer would carry out the order."

Twenty-five-year-old New Yorker Fred G. Bond spent the summer and fall of 1877 hunting buffalo and prospecting in Montana. He returned to the Cantonment on Tongue River shortly before the Nez Percé prisoners' arrival to become one of the captains responsible for conveying the Nez Percés to Fort Buford in western North Dakota. Bond commanded a thirty-two-foot-long, eight-foot-wide boat built of whip-sawed lumber, calked with pitch and tar, which had four-foot sweep oars and to which he later added a sail.

Onto Bond's boat were crowded Colonel Miles, an army doctor, and twenty-two Nez Percés along with rations: salt pork, sugar, coffee, hardtack, navy beans, rice, flour, and baking powder. The boatman negotiated the first stretch of white water safely but watched the rapids overwhelm one craft following him. As the current stuck the vessel broadside, "I knew they would perish," he said. Although Miles told Bond to stop and assist those who had been pitched into the river, none of the Indians survived.

Two days down the river, the boats overtook the soldiers escorting Joseph and the Nez Percés with him. Here Miles and the doctor left the river and joined the mounted party, which was traveling steadily over a rough track. Most of the Nez Percés were riding in wagons, since most of their saddles, tack, and animals had been left at the Cantonment. As Joseph lamented, "Somebody has our horses."

With Miles no longer a part of the river flotilla, the voyage to Fort Buford became a race with Fred Bond in the lead. He organized his captives by enlisting the aid of an older man, whom he called Chief George Washington, to serve as interpreter and hunter and entrusted the Indian with his only gun to kill deer and sage grouse for fresh meat. The women cooked the provisions and gathered red, ripe bull berries to enhance their diet. An old woman Bond called Shades of Night became a lookout while younger boys and one young woman operated the oar sweeps. Bond and the Indians arranged rocks in the bottom of the boat, covered them with sand, and built a fire for warmth and to brew coffee as cold winds blew in from the northwest and slush began clogging the river.

The Yellowstone merged with the muddy, icy Missouri just above Fort Buford and Bond had Chief Washington fire the gun three times to alert the fort so men were on hand to catch the rope the boatman threw ashore. Once Bond unloaded the people, he walked up the incline from river to fort, entered the heavy gates, and sought out the commanding officer.

Having safely delivered his human cargo, Bond intended to collect his pay and return to the Cantonment, but the officer told him there were new orders to take the Nez Percés on to Fort Abraham Lincoln, another two hundred miles downriver. Bond refused to proceed unless he received more pay, whereupon the officer-of-the-day placed him under arrest. Before being jailed, Bond visited "Haybag Row," a string of bungalows where lived married and single women who cooked and did laundry for the soldiers. There he bought all the bread he could find, and he took the food to the Indians and told them to let the other boat captains know he was "striking" for more pay before continuing on to Fort Lincoln.

Days later Bond's pay raise was granted. He repaired the boat he had christened *The Leader*, bought more bread, cakes, pies, potatoes, and vinegar, loaded his people, and pushed into the river for the next leg of the journey.

As Bond continued down the Missouri, Chief Washington killed antelope, women fished, and young boys with newly fashioned bows and arrows killed beaver for their succulent tails. The weather continued colder and ice chunks struck the boat and threatened to close the river to all travel for the season.

Meantime, riding nearly 400 miles from the Cantonment at Tongue River to Fort Abraham Lincoln in North Dakota, Joseph and Colonel Miles established a bond that would endure twenty-five years. Joseph had learned to trust the man into whose custody he had surrendered his people; Miles respected the Nez Percés, calling them "the boldest men and best marksmen of any Indians I have ever encountered." Of their leader he said, "Chief Joseph is a man of more sagacity and intelligence than any Indian I have ever met."

Miles and the soldiers guarding the Nez Percés watched as Joseph, relying on sign language, recounted the recent war to the hundreds who gathered along the Missouri in North Dakota near Fort Berthold, the agency headquarters for the Mandan, Arikara, and Hidatsa tribes. His powerful message left observers stunned at its eloquence even though he uttered not a word. Like Miles, the troops traveling with Joseph and his people later called them the "finest Indians America has produced" and referred to the war against them as "a black page in our history."

Near Fort Lincoln, headquarters of the Seventh Cavalry, the Nez Percés traveling the river route became quiet and gloomy. Bond tried to cheer them, but to no avail. Three long blasts from the Northern Pacific Railroad train heralded the Nez Percés' arrival. Bond wrote: "I was trying to explain to my people that there was the Iron horse and just then the Iron horse let a snort and commenced backing scareing my people and then the great gun at the fort cracked. My poor people fell on their knees." As he maneuvered the boat to the landing, the Indians began a death chant. Later Bond learned that while they were at Fort Buford someone had told the Nez Percés that when the Fort Abraham Lincoln cannon shot twice they would be killed.

In 1877, the Bismarck, North Dakota, main street had wooden sidewalks, false-fronted buildings, and overhanging porches along three business blocks that served rivermen, gamblers, miners, and buffalo hunters. Bond arrived with the first boatload of Nez Percé prisoners in mid-November, and two days later Joseph, riding beside Colonel Miles at the head of the cavalcade, and those who had traveled overland reached the frontier community.

News of the wretched conditions of the Indians, with minimal food and ragged clothing, preceded them. Montana newspapers, since the release of the tourists in Yellowstone, had published articles sympathetic to Joseph and his people, and now Bismarck was ready to welcome them. Residents mobbed the Indians, giving them food as soldiers formed a square around them and a band struck up the "Star Spangled Banner." The women in town even hosted a ball in Joseph's honor, serving salmon to the headman and some of his top warriors to recognize "the admiration we have for your bravery and humanity."

Even General Sherman lauded the Nez Percés, calling their flight "one of the most extraordinary Indian wars of which there is any record." He said, "The Indians throughout displayed a courage and will that elicited universal praise; they abstained from scalping, let captive women go free, did not commit indiscriminate murder of peaceful families which is usual, and fought with almost scientific skill, using advance and rear guards, skirmish-lines and field-fortifications."

Although earlier he had recommended punishment and execution for the headmen and prominent Nez Percé warriors, Sherman had relented on that but now issued new orders sending the Nez Percés to Fort Leavenworth and ultimately to Indian Territory, saying their punishment needed to be extreme, "else other tribes alike situated may imitate their example."

"When will those white chiefs begin to tell the truth?" Joseph asked when told of the new destination.

A Heavy Stone Upon My Heart

ort Leavenworth defined "hellhole" for Joseph and his people. In a camp two miles from the fort, situated between the Missouri River and a lagoon, the Nez Percés suffered from fevers lurking in contaminated water and from the early-summer plague of mosquitoes that spread malaria through the "miserable, helpless, emaciated specimens of humanity," according to the monthly journal *Council Fire.* This Washington, D.C., publication, advocating Indian rights, said conditions at the Leavenworth camp recalled "the horrors of Andersonville," the notorious Civil War prison.

"We had always lived in a healthy country where the mountains were high and the water was cold and clear," Joseph said. Now his people occupied lodges pitched "on a low river bottom with no water except river water to drink and cook with." The malaria brought on fever, chills, and anemia. Although malaria was treatable with quinine—the bitter medicine made from the pulverized bark of the cinchona tree of Peru—the treatment itself caused nausea, vomiting, skin rashes, and a constant tinnitus. But the Indians received little medical care other than their own traditional remedies, and since they had no experience with malaria, the efficacy of Nez Percé medicine was negligible, and at least twenty-one of them died. "I cannot tell you how much my heart suffered for my people while at Leavenworth," Joseph said. "The Great Spirit Chief who rules above seemed to be looking some other way. He did not see what was being done to my people."

Joseph wrote and spoke no English, yet he petitioned the government, just weeks after his arrival at Leavenworth, demanding that it honor surrender terms and return his people to Idaho. Authorities there, however, had handed down indictments against him and other Nez Percés making it impossible for them to be repatriated without facing prison or execution. Therefore, federal officers justified their next order: relocation of the Nez Percés to Indian Territory to join dozens of other tribes in exile, including the Modocs, forced there in 1873; the Northern Cheyennes under Dull Knife, transported to the territory earlier in 1877; and tribes removed from their homelands decades before, including the Delawares, Cherokees, Choctaws, Creeks, Chickasaws, and Seminoles.

On July 21, 1878, the Nez Percés, now under jurisdiction of the Commissioner of Indian Affairs, were herded onto railroad cars and shipped to Baxter Springs, Kansas, for settlement on a portion of the Quapaw Reservation, which they shared with the Modocs. The heat stifled the adults, prostrated Joseph's wife, and killed three children. At Baxter Springs, many fell desperately ill with malaria and, with no quinine for treatment, more than a quarter of the band perished. Joseph said, "It was worse to die there than to die fighting in the mountains."

Indian Commissioner E. A. Hayt, a fifty-five-year-old New Yorker, met with him in October 1878, and the two rode together across southern Kansas and northeastern Indian Territory in search of a better place for the Nez Percés. Hayt called Joseph "bright and intelligent" and said the headman was "anxious for the welfare of his people." Thus, in June 1879, the Nez Percés moved to northeastern Indian Territory, where the red soil did little to nurture their souls. They called it Eeikish Pah, "The Hot Place," sharing their new reservation with Ponca Indians from Nebraska and watching as they also withered, suffered, and died in heat and from disease. The Nez Percés had only remnants of canvas and a few hides for lodges; there were no permanent structures for homes, and there was little food and no medicine. Since their surrender death had claimed more than 100 of them.

Joseph, who had told Nelson Miles and General Howard he would fight no more, continued to fight with the only weapon left to him. He sent his first petition seeking relief for the Nez Percés in December 1877, appealed to Commissioner Hayt in the fall of 1878, and in early 1879 took his cause to a new level: Washington, D.C. There he stepped up to the podium in the court of public opinion seeking justice and reform, and for the rest of his life he would remain relentless in the pursuit of better conditions for his people and a return to the Wallowa Valley. Of his unrelenting campaign Howard eventually told him, "You, Joseph, will show yourself a truly great man, and your people can never be blotted out."

In January 1879, with the interpreter Ad Chapman, who had accompanied the Nez Percés to Indian Territory, and Yellow Bull, one of the most powerful warriors of his tribe, Joseph rode the train to Washington. The Bureau of Indian Affairs Inspector, General John O'Neill, arranged the trip and helped place him on the national stage by setting up interviews with President Rutherford Hayes, Secretary of the Interior Carl Schurz, and various congressmen. In Washington, the headman gave the second most important speech of his life, and O'Neill may have orchestrated it, although Joseph had other supporters at high levels of government, including Indian Commissioner Hayt and Colonel Nelson A. Miles. O'Neill and other supporters informed Joseph that this public opportunity to present his side of the story could help the Nez Percés return to their homeland.

Wearing moccasins, cloth leggings, multiple-loop necklaces, and a blanket coat, Joseph posed for a studio photograph, and he may have worn similar clothing to Lincoln Hall at the corner of Ninth and D Streets on January 14. There for two hours he shared an impassioned message, with Chapman interpreting the Nez Percé language to an audience of diplomats, congressmen, and prominent Washingtonians. Joseph's earlier surrender speech and reports of his reception in Bismarck, North Dakota, had been published in newspapers throughout America, making his name recognizable and ensuring a large crowd for the address. In April 1879, the prestigious *North American Review* published the speech. Newspapers ran excerpts of it and portions of the text appeared on April 5 in *The Idaho Avalanche* under the title "Chief Joseph's Story."

"My friends," he began, "I have been asked to show you my

heart. My name is Hin-mah-too-yah-lat-kekt. I am chief of the Wal-lam-wat-kin band of Nez Percés. Our fathers gave us many laws, which they had learned from their fathers. They told us to treat all men as they treated us, that we should never be the first to break a bargain, that we should only speak the truth."

For more than an hour Joseph spoke and Chapman interpreted as the chief recounted Nez Percé contact with explorers Meriwether Lewis and William Clark, missionaries, and government negotiators who prepared the first treaties. He talked of his father's role in treaty councils, of placing poles around their Wallowa territory so whites would not intrude. He spoke of the land itself and its physical and spiritual power for the Nez Percés.

"The measure of the land and the measure of our bodies are the same," he said. "Do not misunderstand me, but understand me fully with reference to my affection for the land. I never said the land was mine to do with it as I chose. The one who has the right to dispose of it is the one who had created it. I claim a right to live on my land, and accord you the privilege to live on yours."

Joseph briefly recounted the recent war, told of the suffering his people endured, and said he had expected Colonel Miles's word at the surrender to be honored. Now he had been advised he could not return to his homeland because white men lived there and the men of his tribe faced legal action in Idaho. "This talk felt like a heavy stone upon my heart," he said. "I cannot understand how the government sends a man out to fight us, as it did Colonel Miles, and then breaks his word."

After delivering his eloquent message, Joseph returned to Indian Territory and joined his people eking out their meager existence as Miles and others, including the Presbyterian Church and eventually, in 1882, the Indian Rights Association, continued to lobby on behalf of the Nez Percés.

In the wake of the Civil War, the Indian Reform Movement organized under President Grant's Peace Policy. Joseph had earlier dealings with that policy when Presbyterian John Monteith assumed control of the Nez Percé agency at Lapwai prior to the war, and Joseph had rejected the religious teachings that came at the price of lost Indian culture. Now, however, Indian reformers became allies of a sort as they worked to effect improved living standards in Indian Territory. Further, the reformers clamored that removal was impractical and that the entire reservation system was rife with corruption and fraud.

Joseph took advantage of his notoriety from the war and used his skills as orator and diplomat to gain support. His account of the injustices his people had endured since the 1863 treaty that had deposed them from the Wallowa Valley gained widespread sympathy from the press and the general public.

Under provisions adopted in late 1878, the Nez Percés were to share the Oakland Reserve in Indian Territory with the Poncas, led by Standing Bear. This tribe had been removed from Nebraska to Indian Territory in 1876, even though Standing Bear staunchly resisted the relocation. He said that during his prior visit to Indian Territory he saw people "without shirts, their skin burned, and their hair stood up as if it had not been combed since they were little children. We did not wish to sink so low as they seemed to be."

Even so, Indian commissioners placed the tribe in Indian

Territory, and by the time Joseph agreed to join them there many Poncas had already died. In early 1879, as Joseph launched his diplomatic and public relations campaign to return home, Standing Bear gathered thirty of his people and, on January 2, fled toward Nebraska, where they were rounded up and imprisoned. The Ponca chief, with support from Thomas Tibbles, the Omaha *World-Herald* editor and a former abolitionist crusader, went to court and won his suit in a United States District Court ruling that declared "an *Indian* is a PERSON within the meaning of the laws of the United States." Further, Indians had the right to "*life, liberty* and the pursuit of happiness" and could not be held in custody for pursuing these constitutional rights. As a result of the ruling, Standing Bear and the Ponca tribal members with him were granted asylum with the Omaha tribe in Nebraska, on a portion of the Ponca homeland.

Even earlier, Northern Cheyennes under Dull Knife, who had been forced to Indian Territory after the devastating attack on their Wyoming village in November 1876, took flight. Like the Poncas and Nez Percés, the Northern Cheyennes also succumbed in the hot and humid climate. On September 9, 1878, Dull Knife, with nearly 300 followers, broke from the reservation and fled toward Montana. A series of engagements with frontier army troops followed, leading to the capture of the Cheyennes and their incarceration at Fort Robinson in western Nebraska. Still determined to live free or die, the Cheyennes escaped from Fort Robinson in early 1879, but troops pursued and killed most of them. The survivors eventually negotiated for lands in Montana, but only after many had died in their escape toward home.

Undoubtedly these efforts by the Poncas and Northern

Cheyennes affected Joseph and were elements in his motivation to visit Washington and share his concerns with a public audience, since in both cases the surviving Indians were allowed to remain in or near ancestral lands. Joseph, who had eluded frontier soldiers once—for four months and crossing nearly 1,500 miles—knew the devastating consequences. He would not subject his people to flight again.

In October 1877, White Bird and other Nez Percés who had survived the Bear's Paw battle found Sitting Bull's camp in Saskatchewan. The climate there was similar to that of the Nez Percé homelands, but the escapees arrived with no camp supplies or lodges and sparse clothing. The Lakotas shared from their own meager resources, but food sources could barely sustain both the Lakotas under Sitting Bull and White Bird's Nez Percés.

At Joseph's request, his cousin Yellow Wolf eluded troops following the surrender at the Bear's Paw battlefield and entered Canada to locate Joseph's first wife, Bear Crossing, and daughter Sound of Running Water. By early 1878, many Nez Percés in Canada were desperately homesick and decided to migrate to Lapwai, but reservation officials arrested most who returned, including Yellow Wolf and Bear Crossing, and exiled them to Indian Territory. The officials forced Joseph's daughter to remain in Idaho. She lived with relatives, took the name Sarah, and in 1879 married a Nez Percé at Lapwai. Other refugees found sanctuary with Indian tribes and bands throughout the Northwest and Canada and in some cases remained in self-imposed exile for years.

White Bird rejected appeals from Colonel Miles that he

join Joseph in Indian Territory and remained in Canada for the rest of his life, finally resettling near Pincher Creek just east of the Continental Divide in Alberta. In 1892, he was murdered there by a Nez Percé in retribution for the deaths of two children the headman, who was also a healer, had tried unsuccessfully to cure. The killing of a healer under such circumstances was a culturally accepted practice of the tribe.

Joseph's band scratched out subsistence in Indian Territory, affected by drought, livestock theft, and land encroachments. The band had been "issued" ninety-six heifers and four bulls and their agent called them "natural herders," showing "more judgment in the management of their stock than any other Indians I ever saw." Livestock breeding was almost inherent to the Nez Percés, skills learned from generations of breeding horses. Officials also introduced other practices that would help the Indians adjust to reservation life. Joseph's nephew James Reuben came to Indian Territory in 1879, bringing education to the children and the principles of Christianity that his side of the family, living at Lapwai, had long embraced.

Expect the Rivers to Run Backward

I ndian agents watched as the Nez Percés suffered and died in Indian Territory, and began urging their superiors and Congress to take action. Although conditions had improved, still the elders and babies died, including Joseph's youngest daughter. "Such a people should not be allowed to perish," wrote Ponca Agent T. J. Jordan, who also served the Nez Percés. "This great government can afford to be generous and just." The dignity Joseph and his people displayed in the face of intolerable living conditions impressed Jordan, who called them "brave, energetic, exemplary, and faithful."

Agents serving the Nez Percés had taken up their cause, but it was the promotion of Nelson Miles to brigadier general, in 1880, and his assignment as Commander of the Department of the Pacific that made it possible for the Nez Percés to return to Idaho. Miles backed Joseph's claim that the Indian surrender entitled them to again live in their homeland.

"The deep-rooted love for the 'old home' can never be eradicated," Indian Commissioner Hiram Price said in 1882 when he recommended that widowed women be allowed to return to Lapwai. "Any longer delay is in my judgment futile and unnecessary. These people have exhibited a quiet and un-murmuring submission to the inevitable, and have manifested a conscientious desire to obey all laws and regulations pro-vided for their government, yet as each year passes numerous petitions and urgent requests come from them praying to be returned to their old home and relatives."

In the spring of 1883, teacher James Reuben accompanied twenty-nine widows from Indian Territory to Idaho. No fed-eral funds had been appropriated for their train tickets and expenses, so the women sold handicrafts and accepted dona-tions to earn the $1,625 they needed.

Kate McBeth, an austere, heavy set forty-nine-year-old Presbyterian missionary who taught sewing and domestic skills to women on the reservation at Lapwai, joined "gaily dressed" Nez Percé women near the mission church to wait for those returning from Eeikish Pah. The exiles had de-trained near Boise and ridden horses the final 250 miles of their journey. Reuben, wearing a dark blue suit, pistol, and cartridge belt, led the entourage of "the weariest, dustiest, most forlorn band of women" as they halted in a semi-circle facing the agent's office at Lapwai. Reuben addressed the crowd; then the women dismounted and greeted friends and relatives with "weeping and wailing in remembrance of the graves" in Indian Territory, McBeth said.

When this transfer occurred, it breathed new hope into Joseph that all of his people would someday be returned to their country. "You may as well expect the rivers to run backward as that any man who was born a free man should be contented while penned up and denied liberty to go where he pleases," he said. "I only ask of the Government to be treated as all other men are treated. If I cannot go to my own home, let me have a home in some country where my people will not die so fast."

Petitions filed by Indian reformers and citizens from Kansas to Connecticut, including the widow of President James Garfield, took up the Nez Percé cause, pressuring Congress to act. Finally opposition from representatives in western states fell aside and in May 1884 the U.S. Senate approved an appropriation bill that would repatriate the Nez Percés. However, there was no immediate move, leading John W. Scott, then the agent for the Nez Percés, to write: "They are extremely anxious to return to their own country. There is a tinge of melancholy in their bearing and conversation that is truly pathetic."

On April 29, 1885, the federal order finally arrived, and less than a month later the 268 survivors set out in a rainstorm, heading home, the sick and elderly people riding in wagons, most walking thirty miles through the mud to board the train. In Pocatello, Idaho, with the help of a doctor who accompanied them, they eluded a sheriff sent to arrest Joseph for crimes associated with the 1877 war. Farther west the Nez Percés, who had endured seven years of miserable exile, faced yet another stunning blow: not all were destined for the Nez Percé Reservation at Lapwai.

"When finally released from bondage," as Yellow Wolf put it, those who endorsed the Christian religion would settle at Lapwai while those who adhered to traditional, Dreamer, belief would be sent to the Colville Reservation in Washington.

The question, Yellow Wolf said, was "Lapwai and be Christian, or Colville and just be yourself." Only Joseph had no choice. He would be sent to Colville. "But he had the promise that as soon as the Government got Wallowa straightened out, he could go there with his band," Yellow Wolf said.

The band clung to old tribal ways at Colville, hunting, fishing, gathering berries and roots. In ensuing years, agency officials built Joseph a small frame house and a barn, but he preferred his canvas and bark mat lodge. For celebrations and ceremonies the people constructed a longhouse by joining multiple structures. Inside were buffalo robes, bark mats, and three or four fire pits for cooking and heating. The band did not always receive its food and clothing allowance, nor did Joseph's people willingly plant crops, still adhering to the belief that Mother Earth should not be tilled.

In 1887, when Congress approved the Dawes Act, which apportioned Indian lands to individual owners, some Nez Percés took advantage of the provisions and returned to Lapwai for acreage, but Joseph and his most steadfast supporters did not. They could now move to Lapwai, but the Idaho land had never been their home and Joseph held firm to his claim on Wallowa, believing he would one day be allowed to resettle in the land of his younger days. "Never for a moment did his heart turn from his old home to the new one," Kate McBeth said, adding, "The grave of his father was there." Jane Gay, housekeeper for the special agent sent to put Dawes Act provisions into effect in Idaho, said Joseph "will have none but the Wallowa valley. . . . It was good to see an unsubjugated Indian. One could not help respecting the man who still stood firmly for his rights, after having fought and suffered . . . in the struggle for their maintenance."

Joseph traveled to New York City in 1897 at the behest of General Nelson Miles, staying at the Astor House as a guest of former Indian fighter and buffalo hunter turned Wild West showman William F. "Buffalo Bill" Cody, who called the Nez Percé chief "the greatest American Indian ever produced." Joseph, wearing full war regalia, participated in the dedication of Grant's Tomb on April 27, disregarding the fact that it had been President Grant's "Peace Policy" that had forced him from the Wallowa Valley.

On another of his trips east, he visited the Indian boarding school in Carlisle, Pennsylvania, where he saw O. O. Howard and even sat with him for a meal and a photograph. But he resisted the Indian Bureau's efforts to force Nez Percé children to attend boarding schools, where he knew they would be further stripped of their Indian identity and culture. Instead he demanded and got a school at Colville, which he often visited. Even though he seldom liked the teachers sent by the Indian Commission, his solemn presence quieted the children. Occasionally he rebuked a student to pay better attention.

Joseph, whose nine children all preceded him in death, took other youngsters into his home, having close ties with nephews and even welcoming Erskine Wood, the teenage son of Charles Erskine Scott Wood, General Howard's aide-de-camp during the war and the man who recorded Joseph's surrender speech in 1877. This boy spent several months living with Joseph in 1892 and 1893. He hunted pheasant, sage chicken, ducks, and deer, herded Joseph's horses, helped harvest his grain, and joined him in the sweat house and in taking hot water baths by banking rocks to create a basin of water in the river and then adding hot stones to the pool. "He was the kindest of fathers to me, looking after me, providing for me, . . . sometimes gently rebuking me," young Wood said.

As the lad prepared to leave the Nez Percé's lodge for the final time, he asked if his father could do anything for the headman. Joseph said he would like a fine stallion to breed his mares and improve bloodlines. "I looked on Joseph as such a great man, a noble chief driven out of his ancestral home, I revered him so, that I thought his request for a stallion was too puny—was beneath him," Wood said. He told Joseph that kind of request was not what his father had in mind, although later he realized how great a gift it would have been: "Just because I exalted him so high I deprived him of it, and it is something I shall always regret."

The eastern visit in 1897 and Nelson Miles's continuing support and influence led to a governmental investigation into whether the Nez Percé people could resettle in their homeland, and in 1900 Joseph returned to the Wallowa Valley with Indian Agent John McLaughlin to explore the possibility of developing a reservation there. Sobs tore through Joseph's body, now heavy from his sedentary life, when he stood over the grave of his father. "I buried him in that beautiful valley of winding waters," Joseph said. "I love that land more than all the rest of the world. A man who would not love his father's grave is worse than a wild animal."

Despite his reverence for it, and his determined belief that he would again have a place there, federal authorities denied Joseph's request for a Wallowa reservation. Supported by residents of the area, federal authorities would not even allow him to purchase land there for his people.

Still he tried. In Washington in 1903, he presented his case for the Wallowa Valley over a shared meal of buffalo with President Theodore Roosevelt. Joseph appealed to residents and university students in Seattle. He had backing from influential men who admired his grit and determination, but with the goal unachieved, he died on September 21, 1904, in his lodge at Colville. The reservation doctor later said Joseph died of a broken heart.

Let Me Be a Free Man

ost of Joseph's people were picking hops far from Colville when he died. Henry M. Steele, a sub-agent on the Colville Reservation assigned to teach farming to them, had often smoked Joseph's catlinite pipe, inlaid with lead and abalone shell, in friendship with the headman.* Steele took charge of the chief's burial at noon the day following his death with assistance from older Nez Percés and said he felt "whole-souled grief" at the loss of a dear friend. When the body had been interred, mourners placed a small bell on a tall, thin hemlock pole planted at the grave in recognition of Dreamer beliefs that its sound would guide Joseph to the spirit land.

Reports of his death quickly spread across the nation. Men who had supported his efforts to return to the Wallowa Valley considered taking him there after death, but the Nez Percés

---

*Joseph's pipe is in the artifact collection at the Nez Percé National Historical Park in Spalding, Idaho.

decided Joseph should remain at Colville, holding a separate service for him in June 1905, when they dedicated a monument in his honor.

There remained one important Indian ceremony to honor the fallen leader, the potlatch, a two-day distribution of his possessions and food and household goods that belonged to his wives. Yellow Bird, one of the tribe's respected elders, presided along with the nearly blind old Yellow Bull. Present in the council lodge were Joseph's wives, his three nephews, Tow-at-Way of the Umatilla reservation in Oregon, Ollokot of Montana, and Black Eagle from Lapwai, plus women, children, and all the men of his band wrapped in brightly colored blankets and seated upon mats made of woven reeds. Hour by hour the gifting continued with Joseph's war garments and weapons bequeathed to the nephews.

Those present shared a feast in solemn reverence for the life of a great leader. During the monument dedication, Yellow Bull, wearing Joseph's eagle feather war bonnet and astride Joseph's horse, circled the council lodge three times, then said, "Joseph is dead, but his words will live forever."

Joseph's words of surrender at the Bear's Paw are quoted often, but he is known also for his aphorisms, such as these included in his obituary in the *New York Sun*: "Big name often stands on small legs," "Finest fur may cover toughest meat," "Cursed be the hand that scalps the reputation of the dead," and "Look twice at a two-faced man." Joseph's first major public speech in Washington, D.C., in 1879, resounds with his philosophy of life: "Let me be a free man—free to travel, free to stop, free to work, free to trade where I choose, free to choose my own teachers, free to follow the religion of my fathers, free to think and talk and act for myself."

There were later efforts to have Joseph's body returned to the Wallowa Valley, but exhumation plans were rejected by the members of his tribe at Colville who remembered that the grave of Joseph's father at Wallowa had been desecrated. To better protect them, Old Joseph's remains were eventually moved to a new site near Joseph, Oregon, a place revered by Nez Percés and marked by prayer bundles and tokens; Joseph's grave was left on the Colville Reservation.

In 1965, the National Park Service began protecting the sites where important battles and incidents took place during the Nez Percé conflict, eventually designating thirty-eight places in Oregon, Idaho, Montana, Washington, Wyoming, and Yellowstone National Park as part of the Nez Percé National Historical Park and Trail.

In September 1997, 120 years after they were forced to leave, the Nez Percés, with private and federal funding, purchased 160 acres of ground just outside the town of Wallowa, Oregon. The site has grown to 320 acres with a permanent dance arbor and a hiking trail to a point that overlooks the valley so beloved by Joseph. Eventually it will be the location of the Wallowa Band Nez Percé Trail Interpretive Center.

Finally, Joseph's people have a piece of their homeland.

Epilogue

oseph's life spanned a cataclysmic period in American history. His birth in the Wallowa Valley of Oregon barely predated the great American overland migration that resulted in white settlement of the Oregon country. During early childhood he and his family embraced the changes coming when they lived at the Spalding Mission in Idaho and learned English and Christian ways in the classroom of Eliza Spalding. Then, as it became clear that such influences would strip from the Nez Percés their own culture and beliefs, Joseph's father rejected mission life and teachings and instilled in him a love of homeland and Indian tradition that would carry the young man through adolescence and into manhood.

The Christian missions were abandoned by 1855 when the first of several treaty councils took place leading to escalating encroachment onto Nez Percé lands by white settlers. The discovery of gold and an influx of miners, combined with spiritual discord among the Indians, led to the final, irrevocable split within the Nez Percé tribe as Joseph's father and other traditionalists broke away from the Christian influences on the reservation and refused to sign new treaties usurping their lands. At the time of this fracture of the Nez Percé nation, the United States was embroiled in the Civil War, and once that conflict ended, the American military turned its attention to the "Indian problem" and began forcing tribes onto reservations to clear the way for settlers.

As a tribal leader, Joseph had worked for peaceful resolution to the land ownership question, but in June 1877 young men from the White Bird band of Nez Percés retaliated against whites for past wrongs, setting into motion the events that forced Joseph into a war he did not want that ended in the deaths or exile of most other prominent Nez Percé leaders and Joseph's surrender four months later.

During the Nez Percés' hegira, and in the five decades that followed, the American people believed Joseph was the supreme Nez Percé war chief, ascribing to him a role he did not play. Because the Nez Percé war leaders—Looking Glass, Ollokot, White Bird, and Lean Elk—either died during the war or fled to Canada after it, Joseph became the spokesman and the enduring symbol of the tribe. Following the battles, while he was living in miserable conditions in Indian Territory, his influence expanded as he became a nationally recognized leader for Indian rights. Like the Ponca chief Standing Bear, who had gone to court to assert his constitutional privileges, Joseph sought the same civil liberties other Americans already enjoyed, and his skilled oration helped him achieve them not only for Nez Percés but for all Indians.

Although he had rejected Christianity as antithetical to his traditional beliefs, Joseph accepted the help of Presbyterians and Indian reformers to achieve his ultimate dream of returning to his homeland and took advantage of the political climate of the early 1880s when whites began to atone for wrongs committed against indigenous people.

Joseph's moral character, steadfast belief in the rights of his people, and eloquence raised him to a level other important Indian leaders never reached, as he became a symbol—a hero—not only for his own tribe but for all humanity and the love people have for homeland and freedom.

Uneducated by white standards, he was, nevertheless, brilliantly articulate, speaking with the authority of a natural-born leader and philosopher: "Whenever the white man treats the Indian as they treat each other, then we shall have no more wars. We shall all be alike—brothers of one father and one mother, with one sky above us and one country around us and one government for all. Then the Great Spirit Chief who rules above will smile upon this land and send rain to wash out the bloody spots made by brothers' hands upon the face of the earth."

Joseph spoke Nez Percé or Chinook Jargon, and his words were translated by various individuals before being recorded and published in a variety of sources, including newspapers, government documents, official correspondence of men he met with, annual reports of the War Department and Bureau of Indian Affairs, and treaty council proceedings. While Joseph's speeches were both translated and transcribed prior to publication, those actions were done by different people depending on the circumstances and location, making one thing very clear: the essence of his message in all cases is what Joseph said, since the tone and style of his statements have a consistency that makes it apparent they came from the same source. Joseph's eloquence is omnipresent.

The Nez Percé Indians by Alvin Josephy (unabridged edition, New York: Houghton Mifflin Company, 1997; originally published by Yale University Press, 1965) is the most comprehensive book available for an overview of the Nez Percé tribe from the days of their first contact with Meriwether Lewis and William Clark through the years of early missionary influence, first treaties, and background to the conflict of 1877. Equally valuable to my research was *Chief Joseph Country* by Bill Gulick (Caldwell, ID: Caxton Printers Ltd., 1981).

Information on the 1877 Nez Percé conflict is well documented in various military and governmental records and correspondence files and was published in newspapers and periodicals of the era from throughout the nation. Books that were particularly helpful to my research included *Nez Percé Summer 1877: The U.S. Army and the Nee-Me-Poo Crisis* by Jerome Greene (Missoula: Montana Historical Society, 2000); *I Will Fight No More Forever: Chief Joseph and the Nez Percé War* by Merrill Beal (Seattle: University of Washington Press, 1963); *Let Me Be Free: A Nez Percé Tragedy* by David Lavender (New York: Doubleday, 1992); *The Flight of the Nez Percé: A History of the Nez Percé War* by Mark H. Brown (New York: G. P. Putnam's Sons, 1967); and *Children of Grace* by Bruce Hampton (New York: Henry Holt and Company, 1994). For additional details, I used Fred G. Bond's *Flatboating on the Yellowstone, 1877,* published in 1925 by the New York Public Library; an excerpt of a letter from General William T. Sherman to General Philip Sheridan, included in the Sladen Family Papers of the U.S. Army in Carlisle, PA; "An Incident of the Nez Percé Campaign" by H. J. Davis published in *Journal of the Military Service Institution of the United States,* May–June 1905; and *Nez Percé Joseph: An Account of His Ancestors, His Lands, His Confederates, His Enemies, His Murders, His War, His Pursuits and Capture* by O. O. Howard (Boston: Lee and Shephard Publishers, 1881).

For the Nez Percé perspective of the war, like every other person who writes of Joseph and his times I owe a tremendous debt to Lucullus McWhorter, who interviewed Nez Percé survivors, visited important sites with Indian guides, and later wrote two incredibly rich books, *Hear Me, My Chiefs! Nez Percé History and Legend* (1952, reprinted 2000) and *Yellow Wolf: His Own Story* (1940, reprinted 2000), both published by Caxton Printers Ltd., (now Caxton Press) in Caldwell, Idaho. Caxton Press editor Wayne Cornell provided research assistance and permission to quote from those books as well as from *Dreamers: On the Trail of the Nez Percé* by Martin Stadius (Caxton Press, 1999) and *Adventures in Geyserland* by Heister Dean Guie and Lucullus Virgil McWhorter (Caxton Printers Ltd., 1935).

For additional Indian perspective I used *I Will Tell of My War Story: A Pictorial Account of the Nez Percé War* by Scott M. Thompson (Seattle: University of Washington Press in association with the Idaho Historical Society, 2000).

I sincerely appreciate the people and resources of the Montana Historical Society in Helena, Montana. The staff there, particularly Charlene Porsild, director of research, went out of the way to provide access to newspaper articles and documents and to answer my questions. I thank MHS for permission to quote from materials in their vertical files and including documents written by Henry Buck (Small Collection 492), William Moelchert (SC 491), James Boyd (SC 2083), John Samples (SC 715), Lieutenant Thomas Mayhew Woodruff (SC 18), Thomas Sherrill (SC 739), C. A. Woodruff (SC 1326), Nelson A. Miles (SC 923), and O. O. Howard (SC 2315).

Clark Whitehorn, editor of *Montana, the Magazine of Western History*, directed me to important research materials including the following articles from his publication: "Yellowstone Tourists and the Nez Percé" by Mark H. Brown, Vol. 16, No. 3, July 1966; "Where Did the Nez Percés go in Yellowstone in 1877" by William L. Lang, Vol. 40, No. 1, Winter 1990; and "The Army at the Clearwater" by Jerome A. Greene and "Photojournalism, 1877: John H. Fouch, Fort Keough's First Post Photographer" by James S. Brust, both in Vol. 50, No. 4, Winter 2000.

And I am indebted to the late Dan L. Thrapp's *Encyclopedia of Frontier Biography* for biographical information on so many of the individuals associated with Joseph. I use the University of Nebraska CD-ROM version published in 1995.

I am also grateful to the Oregon Historical Society Press for permission to quote from *Days with Chief Joseph* by Erskine Wood (Corvallis: Oregon Historical Society, 1970) and to the Oregon State University Press for permission to use materials from the excellent guidebook *Following the Nez Percé Trail* by Cheryl Wilfong (Corvallis: Oregon State University Press, 1990).

For opportunities to travel portions of Chief Joseph's trail I am indebted to Chuck Coon and the Wyoming Division of Tourism and to Mary Boyle and Al Cluck representing Travel Montana. For assistance along the Nez Percé National Historical Trail I thank Diane Mallickan and Kevin Peters at Spalding, Idaho, Jon James at the Big Hole Battlefield, and Jim Magera at the Bear's Paw Battlefield.

Finally, I value the research assistance and encouragement provided by James A. Crutchfield, Lori Van Pelt, Terry A. Del Bene, Valerie Sherer Mathes, Marc Otte, Bill Groneman, Charlotte Slater, Dr. Diane Noton, the Idaho State Historical

Society, and my family. For permission to use the John Fouch photograph of Chief Joseph I thank Dr. James S. Brust. I especially value the efforts of my editor, Dale L. Walker, who provided so much guidance, and thank Nat Sobel and Tom Doherty, who gave me this opportunity to tell the story of a remarkable American.

OTHER SOURCES

Chalfant, Stuart A., and Verne F. Ray. *Nez Percé Indians.* New York: Garland Publishing, Inc., 1974.

Clark, Ella E. *Indian Legends from the Northern Rockies.* Norman: University of Oklahoma Press, 1966.

Fenn, Elizabeth A. *Pox Americana: The Great Smallpox Epidemic of 1875–82.* New York: Hill and Wang, 2001.

Frazer, Robert W. *Forts of the West.* Norman: University of Oklahoma Press, 1965.

Gay, E. Jane. *With the Nez Percés, Alice Fletcher in the Field, 1889–92.* Lincoln: University of Nebraska Press, 1981.

Gidley, M. *Kopet: A Documentary Narrative of Chief Joseph's Last Years.* Seattle: University of Washington Press, 1981.

Haines, Francis. *Red Eagles of the Northwest.* Portland, OR: The Scholastic Press, 1939.

McBeth, Kate. *The Nez Percés since Lewis and Clark.* Moscow: University of Idaho Press, 1993, from the original published by Fleming H. Revell Company, New York, 1908.

Robertson, R. G. *Rotting Face: Smallpox and the American Indian.* Caldwell, ID: Caxton Press, 2001.

Scott, Douglas D. *A Sharp Little Affair: The Archaeology of the Big Hole Battlefield. Reprints in Anthropology Vol. 45.* Lincoln, NE: J&L Reprint Company, 1994.

Scott, Hugh L. *Some Memories of a Soldier.* New York: Century Company, 1928.

Unruh, John D., Jr. *The Plains Across: The Overland Emigrants and the Trans-Mississippi West, 1840–60.* Urbana: University of Illinois Press, 1979.

Walker, Dale L. *Pacific Destiny.* New York: Forge Books, 2000.

Walker, Deward E., Jr., Vol. Ed. Sturtevant, William C., Gen. Ed. *Handbook of North American Indians, Vol. 12, Plateau.* Washington, DC: Smithsonian Institution, 1998.

Wharburton, Lois. *The Importance of Chief Joseph.* San Diego: Lucent Books, 1992.

The author is grateful for permission to reprint excerpts from the following material:

Carpenter, Frank D. [Guie, Heister Dean, and McWhorter, Lucullus V.] *Adventures in Geyser Land*. Caldwell, ID: Caxton Printers Ltd. (now Caxton Press), 1935.

McWhorter, Lucullus V. *Hear Me, My Chiefs! Nez Percé Legend and History*. Caldwell, ID: Caxton Printers Ltd. (now Caxton Press), 1952 (reprinted, 2000).

McWhorter, Lucullus V. *Yellow Wolf: His Own Story*. Caldwell, ID: Caxton Printers Ltd. (now Caxton Press), 1940 (reprinted, 2000).

Montana Historical Society Archives:

James Boyd. Small Collection 2083. "Reminiscence of James Boyd."

Henry Buck. Small Collection 492. "The Story of the Nez Percé Campaign During the Summer of 1877."

O. O. Howard. Small Collection 2315. Report of Brig. Gen. O. O. Howard, Headquarters Department of the Columbia, January 8, 1876.

Nelson A. Miles. Small Collection 923. Report of Nelson A. Miles, U.S. War Department of Dakota, December 27, 1877.

William Moelchert. Small Collection 491. Letter to David Hilger, November 13, 1827.

John Samples. Small Collection 715. Letter, November 25, 1927.

Thomas Sherrill. Small Collection 739. "The Battle of the Big Hole As I Saw It," 1916.

C. A. Woodruff. Small Collection 1326. Woodruff speeches, "Battle of the Big Hole."

Lieutenant Thomas Mayhew Woodruff. Small Collection 18. Letter.

Stadius, Martin. *Dreamers: On the Trail of the Nez Percé*. Caldwell, ID: Caxton Press, 1999.

Wilfong, Cheryl. *Following the Nez Percé Trail*. Corvallis, OR: Oregon State University Press, 1990.

Wood, Erskine. *Days with Chief Joseph*. Corvallis, OR: Oregon Historical Society, 1970.

Candy Moulton is the author of several books on Western history, including *Everyday Life Among American Indians from 1800 to 1900*, *The Writer's Guide to Everyday Life in the Wild West from 1840 to 1900*, *Roadside History of Wyoming*, and *Wagon Wheels: A Contemporary Journey on the Oregon Trail*. She is coeditor of *Hot Biscuits: Eighteen Stories by Ranch Women and Men*, a collection of short fiction. Moulton makes her home near Encampment, Wyoming.